Robert Fisher

Flower-Land

An Introduction to Botany

Robert Fisher

Flower-Land
An Introduction to Botany

ISBN/EAN: 9783743349537

Manufactured in Europe, USA, Canada, Australia, Japa

Cover: Foto ©Lupo / pixelio.de

Manufactured and distributed by brebook publishing software (www.brebook.com)

Robert Fisher

Flower-Land

FLOWER-LAND:

AN

INTRODUCTION TO BOTANY.

By ROBERT FISHER, M.A.,

*Late Scholar of Sidney Sussex College, Cambridge;
Vicar of Sewerby, Yorks.*

ILLUSTRATED.

London:
BEMROSE & SONS, 23, OLD BAILEY; AND DERBY.

1889.

PREFACE.

THE reception given last year to "Flower-Land" (Part I.), and enquiries for a Hand-book upon a similar plan which should be a little more advanced, cause me to hope that "Flower-Land" in its new and enlarged form, may find some readers and be of use to them. Part I. is revised, and illustrations have been added; Part II. is now issued for the first time.

There are many who would like to have a sound, though but an elementary, knowledge of Flowering Plants. This, I hope, "Flower-Land" will give them in a readable form: though such readers might omit, at their discretion, the portions mentioned below.*

But the book is also arranged to serve as an introduction to more advanced books for those who wish to enter thoroughly into the wonders and delights of Flower-Land. It will save time and

---

* Chapters 18, 25, 30. Pages 66 to 69, 99 to 103, 108 to 110, 116 to 119, 124 to 127, 137 to 142, 214, 215.

trouble to such readers if they will learn patiently, not hurrying on too fast. If anything is worth doing at all it is worth doing well. Part I. is, I hope, easy for a young child to understand, and it should be learned *thoroughly* before passing on to Part II. The Appendix, so far as it belongs to the chapters on Morphology, might well be left until the chapters are first known.

These first lessons in Botany should also be learned, as far as possible, with the plants which are spoken of in the hands, not only from the book and its pictures. The extra time, and perhaps trouble, which this may cause, will be amply repaid.

A word to the reader, who takes up this book for the sake of others, to teach children about Plants.

Examine the plan of the book in the Table of Contents, and always have, if possible, plants or their parts to illustrate your teaching. This method will, I think, interest the child, and help him to remember. It will be a good plan to read the chapter over beforehand—you will then be able to get specimens of plants you require ready for the lesson; or, if you give the instruction out of doors, which is the best plan, you will be able to walk where they will be most abundantly found. A magnifying glass would make the lessons more interesting. Try to cherish in the child an admiration for the beauty and the wonders of plant life, and a reverence for the great Creator.

R. F.

Sewerby, Yorks.,
    July, 1889.

CONTENTS.

	PAGE
PREFACE	iii

PART I.

CHAPTER   I.—Introductory—Flowering Plants 1

PARTS OF A PLANT.

CHAPTER	II.—Flower—Calyx and Corolla	4
,,	III.—Flower—Stamens and Pistil	8
,,	IV.—Root	12
,,	V.—Stem	16
,,	VI.—Leaves	21
,,	VII.—Fruit	26

HOW PLANTS ARE ARRANGED AND NAMED.

CHAPTER VIII.—Classes and Natural Orders	32
,, IX.—Natural Orders—Cross-Bearers and Butterfly Plants	37
,, X.—Natural Orders—Lipped Plants and Umbel-Bearers	41
,, XI.—Genus and Species	46

CHAPTER XII.—Uses of Plants	50
ON COLLECTING AND DRYING PLANTS	53

PART II.

	PAGE
CHAPTER XIII.—A General View	59

MORPHOLOGY.

,,	XIV.—Stems	63
,,	XV.—Roots	70
,,	XVI.—Buds and Branching	76
,,	XVII.—Leaves	83
,,	XVIII.—Different Forms of Leaves	91
,,	XIX.—Leaves (Stipules, Bracts and Scales)	99
,,	XX.—Flowers	106
,,	XXI.—Inflorescence	114
,,	XXII.—The Pistil and its Parts	121
,,	XXIII.—Formation of Seed	128
,,	XXIV.—Fruit	135
,,	XXV.—Different kinds of Fruit	143
,,	XXVI.—Seeds	151
,,	XXVII.—Distribution of Seeds	157

ANATOMY.

,,	XXVIII.—Cells, Vessels, and Tissues	164
,,	XXIX.—Systems of Tissue	171
,,	XXX.—Wood and Bark	175
,,	XXXI.—Contents of Cells and Vessels	183

PHYSIOLOGY.

,,	XXXII.—Absorption and Transpiration	190
,,	XXXIII.—Further changes in the Sap	195
,,	XXXIV.—Growing Plants	201

CLASSIFICATION.

,,	XXXV.—The three Classes	207
,,	XXXVI.—From Class to Natural Order	213
APPENDIX		221
INDEX		231

FLOWER-LAND.

CHAPTER I.

FLOWERING PLANTS.

Fig. 1.—Cowslip (*Primula veris*).

I HEAR that you would like to be a Botanist, and I am going to write you a little book which I hope will help you. You will find a good many pictures in it, and these will make it easier for you to understand what I tell you. But you must not be satisfied with merely looking at the pictures in the book. If you wish to become a good Botanist you must go and find many other pictures for yourself. This will be much the best plan, for first you will have all the fun of looking for them, and then when you have found them, they will be better than any pictures you have ever seen.

You will know that I mean you to go and find the flowers themselves, to admire them, and to see how wonderfully and how differently they are made.

Now, it is a fine day, and the grass is nice and dry, so let us be off upon our first excursion.

Yes, that will do very well for us to begin with. You have found a daisy, or a dead nettle, or a buttercup, or a dandelion, or some other common flower which you know very well. What did you pick it from? Did you not notice?

See, here is another flower. We will stay a little, and find out what it belongs to. It is quite fast, you see, upon its stem, and the stem is held fast to the ground by the root. Now, we will dig it up, and have the *whole plant—flower*, and *leaves*, and *stem*, and *root* together.

As we walk along I can now tell you what it is to be a Botanist. It is to know about plants.

But many plants are very different from this one we have taken up, of which the pretty flower attracted you. On many kinds of plants you would not find these flowers.

We will try and find some of them. Look amongst the grass, or in the ditch, or on the bankside, or on the stones of an old wall, or the trunk of an old tree, and see if you can find some *moss*. That is such a plant as we are looking for; it has no true flowers.

But let us mark the stems of the trees or bushes which are near. There is one that looks quite grey, and indeed on one side it is almost covered with a short, dry, greyish-coloured substance.

We will gather a small piece of it. It is a *lichen*. It is another instance of a plant that has no true flowers.

If we were on the seashore, we should find another instance in the *seaweed*.

Perhaps, if it is autumn, we shall see a *mushroom*, or a *puff-ball*, as we go through the fields; or we may see a heap of toad-stools by the road-side; or a bright red, or white, or yellow substance upon some piece of wood which lies about. Any one of these would be a *fungus*—another kind of plant which has no true flowers.

You may also succeed in finding another example in a *fern*; but though they are so common in some places, in others you may go far and not find one.

But our talk about Botany has been long enough for you to know what it is to be a Botanist. There is enough, and more than enough, in "learning about plants" to give you pleasure all your life long.

To be a Botanist is to be like a traveller, going from country to country, and in each finding new wonders and new beauties.

The mosses, then, the lichens, the seaweeds, the fungi, and the ferns, we call *flowerless plants;* for they have no flowers such as those you know so well.

I shall say no more to you about them for some time. You will learn first about the *flowering plants;* the flowerless plants will remain until you are older.

CHAPTER II.

FLOWER—CALYX AND CORolla.

Fig. 2.—Bulbous Buttercup.
(*Ranunculus bulbosus.*)

I SHALL begin to-day by telling you what a "flowering plant" is. "Oh! I know that," perhaps you say. "It is a plant that has flowers, as a buttercup, a daisy, or a poppy." But I once went out with a little girl to pick some flowers, and she would not have a bit of groundsel; she called it a *weed*, and not a *flower*. So that you may not think so, we will gather a few flowers of different kinds as we go along, and see what a flower really is.

Pick three or four buttercups; choose the tallest you can see, and those which have smooth, round stems, if you can find them. Look for them by the roadside or in the meadow, and gather a few other flowers as well.

Now, I will take a buttercup, a single flower, and hold it by the stalk, upright. What a pretty yellow cup it is! As yellow as butter, is it not? So children hold it to each other's chins, and if it shines they say that they are fond of butter. Shall I try you? But there, I hold it up again.

And now I must tell you rather a long name. This yellow cup is called the *corolla*. (Fig. 3c.) Corolla is a word of a foreign language (Latin), and means "little crown" or "garland."

Have you a cowslip, or a primrose, or a dandelion in your bunch? They have, like the buttercup, the corolla yellow. But look at the daisy—or, have you a piece of May? There it is white. And you have another instance in the snowdrop, which you know so well. Sometimes the corolla is blue, as in the forget-me-not, or the speedwell, or the violet. Sometimes it is red, as in the little pimpernel or the poppy.

If you look over the flowers you have gathered, you will see corollas of different colours, different sizes, and different shapes.

But it is time to tell you of another part of the flower. Let us go back to the buttercup. There is the yellow cup; but a cup should have a saucer. Can we find one? See, I hold the buttercup so that you can look at it from below. What do you see now, just at the top of the stalk, and spreading out under part of the corolla? Five little whitish-yellow leaves.

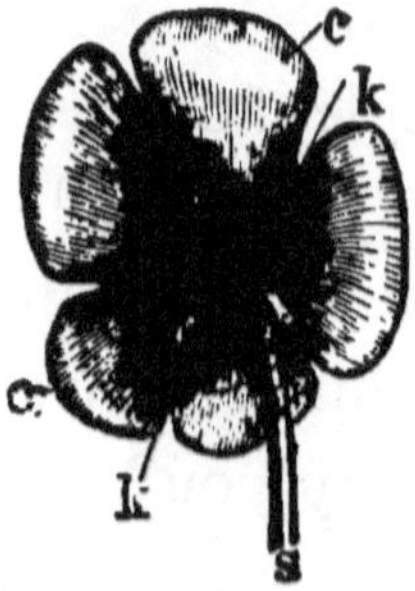

Fig. 3.—Flower of Buttercup. (*ranunculus acris*.) *c* corolla. *k* calyx.

Are they not there? If not, we must take another buttercup flower, and try again. We will choose one that has only just come into blossom. If it is one with the round, smooth stem I spoke of, you will see the saucer-leaves plainly enough. The larger yellow cup is standing in a smaller whitish-yellow saucer. The saucer is called the *calyx*. (Fig. 3k.) If it is very early in the year, perhaps you will not be able to find this buttercup with the spreading calyx. Still the buttercup will have its calyx, though its little leaves instead of being spread out will be turned back close upon the stalk. (Fig. 2.)

Now look for the calyx in your other flowers. You will see it very plainly in the primrose, or wild rose ; and in these it will be green in colour, as it generally is. And do you not remember it in the strawberry? How each strawberry is in its saucer or calyx? (Fig. 24.)

Like the corolla, the calyx differs greatly in size and shape. In the buttercup, the corolla is larger than the calyx, but sometimes the calyx is larger than the corolla. Though you will find both calyx and corolla in most flowers, some have only a calyx or a corolla, and in some the calyx very soon falls off.

Some flowers, too, are very small. If you look carefully you will find several, I dare say, which you did not notice before; but, wherever you find calyx or corolla (or both), however small and insignificant, you have found "a flower."

Fig. 4.
Flower of Mallow.
(*Malva sylvestris*).

There are two other parts of a perfect flower, which we shall learn about next time. Now, let us see if we can tell which is the calyx or corolla in every different kind of flower we can find as we go home (*cf.* Figs. 1, 4, 22, 25).

CHAPTER III.

FLOWER—STAMENS AND PISTIL.

Fig. 5.— Burnet-leaved Rose.
(*Rosa spinosissima.*)

You have already learnt about two of the parts of a perfect flower, the *calyx* and the *corolla;* the calyx holding the corolla as a saucer holds a cup. The other two parts of a flower we shall learn about to-day.

I think our old favourite, the buttercup, will suit us best: it is common everywhere, and we shall soon find one. Yes, here are several, so we will pick that bright one which has just opened.

How pretty it is inside the corolla. Do you see this ring of little yellow things? They are like golden threads with knobs upon the ends of them. If you could see them through a glass, which would make them seem larger, they would be like little yellow bags of dust, each placed upon a stalk. (*cf.* Fig. 23a.)

These are called *stamens*. (Fig. 6.) Rub them with your finger, and you will see upon it the yellow dust from their little bags. Both the bags and the dust which they have in them are very different in shape and size in different kinds of flowers—so also are the stalks on which the bags are placed. In some flowers these little stalks are wanting.

Fig. 6.—A Stamen.

As we go along, we may find a cuckoo-flower, a white dead nettle, a piece of May; or a poppy, foxglove, or wild rose. (Fig. 5.) In any of these you will see the stamens very clearly. In some flowers there are many of them, as in the buttercup; but in some the stamens are few, and they do not always have the bright yellow colour of these we have been looking at in the buttercup.

But there is one more part of the perfect flower for you yet to learn, and it is in the middle of all. This is called the *pistil*—another hard name for you to remember, but it is the last. Like the stamen, the pistil has a kind of bag, or bags, but instead of being at the top, as in the stamens, in the pistil they are at the bottom. (Fig. 7.)

Fig. 7.— A Pistil.

Sometimes a stalk springs from them which is divided, knobbed, or thickened at the top. But with the pistils, as with the stamens, there is a great difference both in shape and size in different kinds of flowers. Here in the buttercup you can see the pistil, with its many bags, right in the middle of the flower, and surrounded by the stamens; just as the stamens are inside the corolla, and the corolla is inside the calyx.

If you have a primrose, we can find in it a good specimen of a pistil. First I pull off the corolla; it comes away easily enough; and now if you look into the calyx, you can see the knobbed top of the pistil. Let us see more of it. Carefully tear away the calyx from the stalk without injuring the pistil, and you see it all—the little round green bag at the bottom, and from it the slender knobbed stalk like a green and tender pin.

It is in this little bag of the pistil that the seeds of plants are formed; and if you break this one open, you will very likely find some little green things inside it which will gradually ripen into seeds. So also in the pistil bags of an old buttercup flower. If when you get home you can get

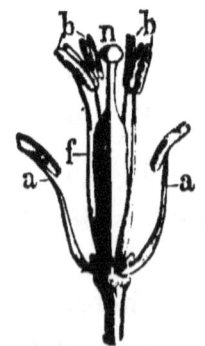

Fig. 8. — Flower of Brassica or Turnip. Corolla removed. *a* and *b*, stamens; *fn*, pistil.

a large white or orange lily from a garden, you will see the stamens and pistil very plainly, and the dust from its stamens is very plentiful; or you can see them plainly in the foxglove, the honeysuckle, the wallflower, the pimpernel, the speedwell, and many others (*cf.* Fig. 8).

In some flowers you will find only stamens or pistils, but not both; just as in some you cannot find both calyx and corolla, but only one of them.

But these are the four parts which make up a perfect flower, and I dare say by this time you know these four hard names quite well—*calyx, corolla, stamens*, and *pistil.*

We will amuse ourselves as we go home by seeing how different these parts are in the different kinds of flowers, and that will help you to remember them.

CHAPTER IV.

ROOTS.

Fig. 9.— Ipecacuanha with ringed root.

FOR our walk to-day we will ask for a trowel or an old blunt knife. Yes; that small trowel will do very well, and as we go I will tell you what we want it for.

You are learning, you know, about *flowering plants*. You have learned something about their flowers, but we have not yet talked about their other parts—roots and stems and leaves. To-day we are going to talk about their roots; and, as we shall want to see them our trowel will be useful in digging them up. For the root, as I dare say you know, is the part of the plant which grows downwards into the ground.

Have you ever seen a tree which has been blown down? Then you can see its roots. How large and strong they are, and how firmly they have fixed themselves in the earth—so firmly that you see a great lot of earth still sticking to them, and quite a large hole in the ground where the tree used to stand. When the wind is very high, and we see the branches of the tall, strong trees bending to and fro, it is the deep, strong roots which hold it in its place so firmly, and make it able to resist the wind.

But the plants we shall look at will not be large ones, like the trees or bushes, but the little ones that we can get at easily, and carry in our hands.

We will begin with a root of common grass. Pick out a single plant as well as you can, and, when you have well loosened the earth all round it, you can lift it gradually root and all. Now, if you shake the earth from it, you will see that it has many *rootlets*. They grow separate from each other from one part of the plant just under the ground; and are like long threads, some of them being again divided into still finer branches. Look for the common groundsel, and compare its root with that of the grass. In the groundsel you can see where the root begins to divide or branch, and how the branches get smaller and smaller

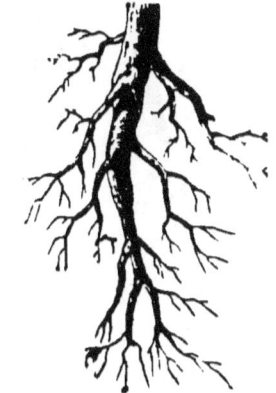

Fig. 10.—A Branching Root.

until they are like little threads. Let us dig up a daisy. It is the same kind of root you see, although its rootlets are a little thicker and not so much divided. (*cf.* Figs. 10, 27.)

In some plants the roots have knobs or swellings in them, sometimes so close together all the way down that they look like strings of beads (Fig. 9). In others the branches of the root are swollen so that they look like a bundle of longish bags, as in the garden dahlia. But let us see what kind of a root this dandelion has. Shall I dig it up for you? It is not easy to get up, its root goes so far into the ground. You see I have broken it; but here is a good piece of the root, and we can see very well what it is like. In some cases it may be forked, and it has little threads growing from it here and there; but it has not separate rootlets from about one centre, or many branchings, like those we have been speaking of. You will know this kind of root very well, for you have often seen it in different shapes in the carrot, the turnip, and the radish (Fig. 11).

Fig. 11.—Root of Beet.

We will look at a few more roots as we go along, though I fear we shall not find a specimen of each of those kinds I have been telling you of. There is, however, one kind that we will particularly look for.

Can you find a wild hyacinth? If not,

a snowdrop, tulip, or large lily from a garden will do as well. In any of these you will find a swelling or bulb, just above the root (Fig. 12). I want you to remember that this bulb is not the root. If you notice any of the plants I have just mentioned, you will see the root, with its many rootlets, growing downwards from the bottom of the bulb. Perhaps at home you have a hyacinth growing in water in a hyacinth glass, or can see one somewhere. If so, you can see how its roots grow very well. (*cf.* Fig. 13).

Fig. 12.—A Bulb.

But do you know what roots are for? What is the use of them? Through the roots liquid food is taken up, and so passes into the plant. You will be able to learn more about this when you are older. But you can remember now that roots are not only meant to fix plants firmly in the ground, but more especially to help to feed them and make them grow.

CHAPTER V.

STEMS.

Fig. 13.—Saffron Crocus.
(*Crocus sativus*).

WE shall not want our trowel to-day, for I shall not tell you any more at present about *roots*, which grow downwards into the earth.

I am going to talk to you about that part of a plant which grows above the ground, and bears leaves and flowers—it is called the *stem*.

There are, indeed, some stems which are partly or altogether under the ground. You will see something of the kind in the primrose. These underground stems send out roots downwards, and leaves and flowers upwards. In the wood anemone they creep along just under the ground.

If we can find any, we will loosen the earth with a stick, and with care we shall get a piece two or three inches long, and have a good specimen of one of these underground stems. They have a special name, and you will learn more about them when you get older.

But I dare say you have planted snowdrop or tulip bulbs in your garden. From the bottom of the bulb the root grows downwards; from the top of it, the stem pushes its way upwards; and at last expands into leaves and flowers (*cf.* Fig. 13).

Some day you must dig up a daffodil or blue-bell (hyacinth) or snowdrop plant, and perhaps you will be surprised to find how deep it is in the earth.

The next time you see an onion bed, if the onions are large enough, you will see an example of a stem swollen at the bottom (a *bulbous* stem), which is all above the ground.

We will look amongst the grass for some common white clover. Now, follow its stem, and see how it trails along the ground. It has a *creeping* stem. You can see it again in this other kind of clover, which has little round heads of yellow flowers about as big as peas.

A plant with a little dark blue flower, common by hedgesides, is such a good example of this kind of stem that it is called Ground Ivy or Gill-run-along-the-ground (Fig. 14). We shall be sure to find plants with creeping stems.

Can we find any with *climbing* stems? The large white convolvulus is one of them; so are the hop and the honeysuckle. If we see any of these, we will stop and notice how they twist and climb round anything to which they are near. There is a tree with some ivy growing up it, and the ivy will do very well for our example of a plant with a climbing stem.

The long twining arms, into which the branches of some plants grow, and by which they climb, are called *Tendrils*. You can see them very well in the Vine tree, upon which grow the beautiful grapes.

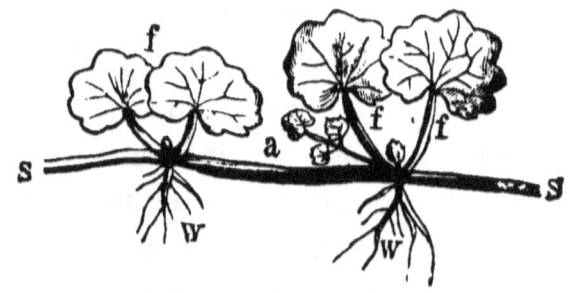

Fig. 14.—Ground Ivy.
(*Nepeta* (*Glechoma*) *hederacea*).

Our old favourite, the buttercup, is here in plenty. It is as good an instance as we can have of the common branched and *upright* stem. We have it in a larger size in the oak, the ash, and other trees.

In the buttercup the stem is soft and juicy. Plants with this kind of stem are called *herbs*, and their stems *herbaceous*.

In the ash a great part of the stem is hard, and plants with this kind of stem are called *bushes*, or *trees*, and their stems *woody*. The outside covering or skin of this kind of stem is called *bark*.

Now, if we notice the stems or *trunks* of the trees, we shall find some of them with rough bark, like the oak or elm; and some of them with smooth bark, like the ash or beech.

The stems of herbs also are rough or smooth. We will bend down this stinging nettle with my stick, and look at its stem; it is one of those stems which have hairs on them. Some stems, as in the wild rose, have *prickles* (Fig. 5); some, as in the hawthorn, have *thorns*.

Then some are round, some are square, and some are *hollow* in the middle. We will try the stems of a few of the taller herbs we see, and shall very likely find a hollow one. One plant with a hollow stem is very common in woods and hedgerows—it is two or three feet high, has very divided leaves, and clusters of little white flowers. But you will know an elder bush if we can find one. If we cut off a branch, we shall find that the middle of it is filled with a soft substance called *pith;* and, as country boys know very well, a piece of elder with its pith cleared out makes a very good popgun.

In trees like the oak, and ash, and elm, however, it is not so. I expect you have often seen the stem or trunk of one of them which has been cut down. How solid it is, as if it had never had any pith at all!

What a great many different kinds of stems there are! You will find them very interesting when you are able to know more about them.

The use of the stems is to bear the leaves and flowers. Through the stems, also, the liquid food which is taken up by the roots is carried to all parts of the plant, to nourish it and make it grow.

Let us take a plant stem—a buttercup will do.

Now, if we cut it across and squeeze it, we shall see this liquid food or juice. It is called *sap*.

I shall tell you a little more about how a plant lives and grows when I tell you about the leaves in the next chapter.

CHAPTER VI.

LEAVES.

Fig. 15.—*a*, Spray of the Pea; *b*, a flower; *c*, the stamens; *d*, the fruit (pod).

To-day I am going to tell you about *leaves*.

When you begin to find out the names of plants from the descriptions which are given of them in books you will find the differences between leaves a great help to you. So you must notice both the shape and the surface of leaves, and also how they grow upon the plant.

Look, for instance, at this primrose, or this dandelion plant. All the leaves grow at the very bottom of the stem, just where the stem and the root join. Such leaves are called *root* leaves. (Fig. 1, p. 1.)

In this buttercup you see leaves growing here and there upon the stem. These are *stem* leaves. (*cf* Fig. 2, p. 4.) Stem leaves grow singly, in pairs in rings round the stem, and in other ways. Sometimes they are without any stalks, and pass some way down the stem.

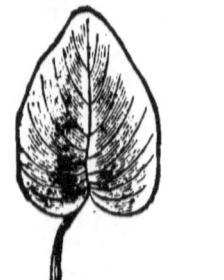

Fig. 16.—A simple leaf; heart-shaped.

But you have to notice the shape and surface of leaves, as well as the way in which they grow upon the plant. So take a buttercup, or a daisy, or a dandelion leaf. You see they are of one single piece. The buttercup leaf is a good deal divided, but still it is all in one piece. These are called *simple* leaves. Figs. 16, 17, 18. (*cf* Figs. 1, 2, 9, 13.)

Fig. 17.—A simple leaf.

But if you now pick a leaf of the ash tree, or the wild rose, or the common clover, you will find it very different. It has several pieces upon its one stalk. A leaf of this kind is called *compound*, and each of its little pieces or little leaves is called a *leaflet*. Fig. 19. (*cf* Figs. 5, 15, 30.)

Fig. 18.—Half a divided but simple leaf.

How beautifully this rose leaf is notched along its edges, the dandelion more irregularly so, the buttercup more irregularly still, but the edge of the daisy leaf is not notched at all.

The general shape of a leaf is also to be noticed. You will find them egg-shaped, heart-shaped (Fig. 16), shield-shaped, fiddle-shaped, and many others.

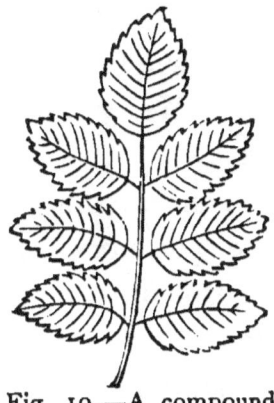

Fig. 19.—A compound leaf.

As for the surface of leaves, sometimes they are smooth and shiny, as in the ivy or the holly; sometimes they are downy, or woolly, or rough with hairs. These hairs are of many kinds, and are found on other parts of a plant besides the leaves. Some of them are hooked, like those of the common Harriff (hair-rough). I dare say you do not know the plant by its name, but perhaps you have found it or its seeds hooked fast to your clothes when you have been walking in a wood, or picking flowers from the hedge-side. Some hairs have little bags belonging to them. In one kind of rose these little bags are scent-bags, so it is called *sweetbriar*. But in the nettle they are poison-bags, and when its little hairs pierce you they sting, as I dare say you know very well.

Now, in the primrose the surface of the leaf is uneven; or if we can see a thistle we shall find that its leaves are quite crumpled, and are also armed with little spines. Can we find a holly bush? But, no doubt, you know what its leaves are like quite well, and have found out when you have been decorating for "Merry Christmas" that they are very prickly also.

Leaves sometimes take the form of *spines*, as in the gorse or furze, the prickly bush which grows on heaths or commons, and has such beautiful yellow flowers.

Sometimes, instead of growing into spines, they grow out into *tendrils* (p. 18). You can see these leaf tendrils upon the plants of the common pea, as they are twined round the pea-sticks in our gardens (*cf* Fig. 15).

You will soon become familiar with these differences in the arrangement, and shape, and surface of leaves, when you learn to make out the names of plants from books in which they are described. But I hope you can now tell me the difference between a *simple* leaf and a *compound* one.

I will tell you as we go home how useful the leaves are in helping the plant to grow. Do you remember how the plant gets any food at all? Yes, you are quite right. Liquid food is taken up from the soil, through the roots, and so passes up into the plant. It is in the sap, which goes up the stem and is spread out through all the leaves.

And through the leaves the plant *breathes*. I wonder if you know what happens when you breathe.

You send out of your body what you do not want, and you take in from the air what you do want. Now there are dotted about upon the leaves a lot of little openings or mouths. You cannot see them without a glass to magnify the leaves—that is, to make them appear larger—but they are there. Through them the plant sends out what it does not want, and takes in fresh nourishment from the air, and the sap carries it away to help the whole plant to grow.

Fig. 20.—Surface of a leaf magnified, showing the openings or mouths.

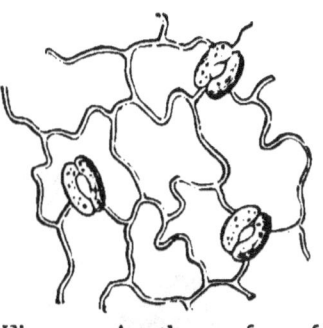

Fig. 21.—Another surface of leaf, more highly magnified.

You will now understand how necessary it is if you have any plants in the house, not only to water them at the roots. If you let them get dusty, the little mouths upon their leaves get choked; so you must take them out now and then, and water them all over. They will enjoy it, and benefit by it, just as you enjoy your cleansing and refreshing bath.

CHAPTER VII.

FRUIT.

Fig. 22.—The Wild Raspberry. (*Rubus idæus.*) *b*, The Fruit.

Do you remember my telling you about the pistil? I showed it to you in the primrose, as well as in the buttercup, and we saw that it had a little bag or bags, from each of which grew up a kind of beak. In the primrose, one bag and a long slender beak; in the buttercup, many bags with short pointed beaks.

Let us look again at the pistil in the buttercup.

We will try and find one that has been some time in flower. Here is one from which calyx, and corolla, and stamens have fallen off, and now you can see the pistil very well. It has many little bags, about 30 or 40 of them, rather flat, with short pointed beaks. You are looking at the *fruit* of the buttercup.

I will break off one or two of the little pistil bags, and place them in your hand. If you look carefully you will see that they are a little swollen in the middle. That is because each little bag has a seed inside it.

Fig 23.—Pistil of Buttercup (magnified). *a,* stamen.

Now, in the buttercup, as we have seen, the fruit is the ripened pistil—a bundle of pointed pistil bags containing the seed. But in other plants these beaked pistil bags are very different. They are found in many different shapes; they are arranged in many different ways. Sometimes they are joined with the calyx and other parts of the flower; in some plants they have one seed, in others many seeds. So we have different kinds of fruits. I will tell you about some of them, and we will see how many different kinds we can find as we go along.

If it is not too late in the year, we may come across some wild strawberries. Well, the strawberry has many separate pistil or seed bags, with single seeds in them, like the buttercup. But they are carried further apart from one another by the sweet juicy pulp which you like so much to eat, and if you look at a straw-

Fig. 24.—Strawberry. Flowers and Fruit.

berry you will see them there. (Fig. 24.)

The wild rose has the same kind of dry pistil or seed bags as the buttercup and the strawberry; only in the wild rose they are all held together and shut up in the tube of the calyx, which swells out so as to hold them, and turns red when ripe. No doubt you have often seen these wild rose fruits. People call them *hips*. If it is late enough in the season I dare say we shall find some of them to-day. If we do, I will cut one open, and you will see the little pistil or seed bags inside.

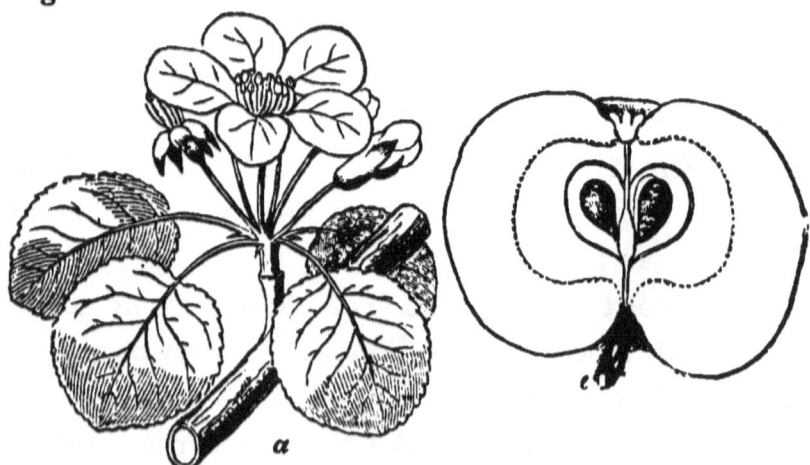

Fig. 25.—Apple Flower, and Fruit cut in half.

The apple is not quite the same. It has several

pistil bags, but they are enclosed in the calyx tube, which swells out all round them into the soft part which you like to eat. The pistil or seed bags are those scaly leaves in the middle, which we call the *core* (Fig. 25).

If we pass through a wood, we may find some wild raspberries (Fig. 22). But here is another fruit of the same kind, the common blackberry. You see, again, a heap of separate pistil bags, as in the buttercup, only in the blackberry the bags swell and grow soft and pulpy. The little beak is a fine hair, and often remains visible when the fruit is ripe.

Can we find a wild cherry, or a sloe, or wild damson? These are plants with only *one* pistil or seed bag instead of many. So their fruit is like one of the pulpy bags we have been looking at in the raspberry or blackberry. It is so much larger that you see better how it is made up. First a soft skin. How beautifully it is coloured! And you can think of the yellow apricots, blue and purple plums, and bright red cherries. Then the juicy pulp. In the middle the hard shell—we call it the stone of the fruit. Inside all, the seed, or, as we say, the kernel.

If we can find a nutbush, with some fruit on it, we shall have another instance of a fruit with a single pistil or seed bag. But in the nut the outside skin of the bag has become hard and brown. The shell covers and keeps safe the seed or kernel.

The fruit of the common pea or bean is another good instance of a single pistil or seed bag. You call it a *pod* (Fig. 15, *d*), and inside you find the peas or beans—its many seeds. We may find examples in the fruit of the vetch, or the gorse.

Now if we could find a poppy, or a foxglove, I could show you another kind of fruit. It is a fruit of many pistils or seed bags, only instead of being separate, as in the buttercup, they are enclosed within a skin or covering. In the poppy, the fruit is like a round parchment box with a flat top to it. When it is ripe, there are holes at the top, out of which you can shake many seeds from the different divisions or bags which are inside (Fig. 26).

Fig. 26.—Fruit of Poppy.

Sometimes fruit of this kind is not altogether dry like the poppy. There is the same arrangement of pistil or seed bags in an outer skin in the juicy fruit you know so well—the orange. I dare say you have often first peeled off the rind or skin, and then separated and eaten one by one the little juicy bags in which you found the pips or seed.

Then there are the berries we know so well, such as the fruit of the currant, grape, or gooseberry.

There are still some other kinds of fruit, and each kind has its own special name, but I only want you to learn now what the fruit of a plant is. It is the seed vessel and its seed. So cucumbers, vegetable marrows, and tomatoes, are fruits, as well as apricots, plums, and grapes.

The fruit is the last part of a plant I have to tell you of, so I will repeat in a few words the chief parts of a plant and what they are for.

The root, stem, and leaves of a flowering plant are the parts by which it grows and brings forth flowers. The flowers in their turn are the parts by which it brings forth its fruit with seeds. Then if you sow the seeds, young plants grow up like the old parent plants; *root* and *stem*, and *leaves* and *flower*, and *fruit* and *seed* again.

CHAPTER VIII.

CLASSES AND NATURAL ORDERS.

Fig. 27.—Part of Foxglove (*Digitalis purpurea*), showing net-veined leaves & root.

You have already learnt something about the chief parts of flowering plants, and about the way in which they grow. I must now tell you something about the way in which they are arranged and named.

When you begin to try and find out the names of plants, you will find that they are arranged, first of all, into three great divisions, which are called *classes*. We shall leave one of them until you are older. The remaining two classes are known from each other by several differences, but at present I will only tell you about two of them.

One difference is in the way the seed begins to grow. Perhaps you have sown mustard seed; and if you have a little garden probably some radish seed as well. When the seed begins to grow it bursts open, and two little leaves, just opposite to each other, open out from it, and at last you see them above the ground. If the mustard is sown rather thick, and with very little fine earth over it, you can generally see these two seed leaves as they begin to push out from the seed.

You can see them also in the springtime under almost any common sycamore or maple tree. Under the tree, or near it, you will generally find some of its seeds, which have begun to grow. The two seed leaves, which have been shut up in their little seed case, gradually push their way out, and as they unroll, the baby sycamore sends out its roots into the ground that it may live and grow. You should try and find some of these sycamore or maple seeds in different stages of growth; from the seed just bursting, until you find the empty seed case, and the young plant fairly started in life, with its seed leaves expanded as you can see it in the picture. Fig. 29,

Fig. 28.—Sycamore or Greater Maple. (*Acer pseudo-platanus.*) *b* the fruit.

(*cf.* Fig. 28 *b*. the fruit or seed-case containing seed).

These seed leaves are not always so easily seen or known. They do not always expand and become green like those you have been looking at, and you must wait until you are older to understand all about them. But plants which begin to grow with two opposite seed leaves belong to one of the two great classes of flowering plants.

In the other class, the seeds have only one seed-leaf instead of two. It is from this difference that these two classes are generally named, but the name is too difficult for you to learn now, though you can remember what the difference is.

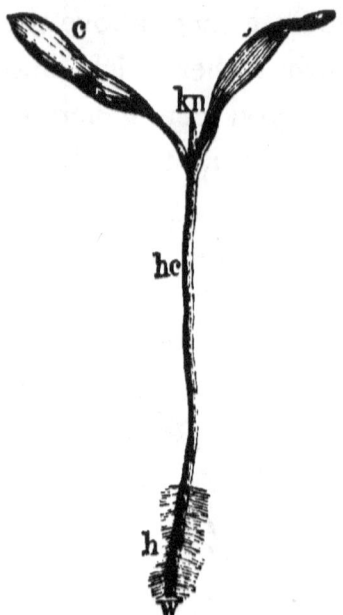

Fig. 29.—Seedling of Maple. *c c* its seed leaves.

I will now tell you of another difference between these two classes of flowering plants—one which is easier for you both to see and to understand—so pick me a leaf or two of the buttercup or dandelion. If you can see a rose bush or an ash tree, one of their leaves will be better still. Now hold the leaf up to the light and see how beautifully its veins are branched and make an irregular kind of network.

These are called *net-veined* leaves. As a general rule plants with these net-veined leaves belong to one of the two great classes of flowering plants (*cf.* Figs. 1, 22, 27).

But now pick a leaf of the wild hyacinth or snowdrop, or, which you are sure to find, a blade, *i.e.*, a leaf of grass. In this leaf you see that the veins run more evenly side by side, and though you may find cross veins in leaves of this kind, yet they never make an irregular branching network. (*cf.* Fig. 169). Leaves of this kind are called *straight-veined*. As a general rule plants with these straight-veined leaves belong to the other of the two great classes of flowering plants. There are a few exceptions to this general rule, but until you learn more about the other differences between the two classes, and about their proper names, you can think of them as the "net-veined" and "straight-veined" classes.

These two classes are then divided again until you have the flowering plants arranged in about one hundred divisions, which are called *natural orders*. You will learn afterwards about the way in which botanists arrange these "natural orders" under *divisions*, and the "divisions" under the two *classes*.

It is the arrangement of plants in their natural orders that I want you to remember. Some of these natural orders are very easy to learn about. I will tell you about a few of them in my next chapter. But as they are known from one another chiefly by the shape of the flower, I will ask you, as we go home, if you can remember what the parts of a flower are.

I will pick this buttercup flower. It has not been open very long, and is a good specimen, so all the parts of the flower are here. And now see if you can tell me them by name. Yes! Outside of all the calyx, then the bright yellow corolla, then these many little stamens, and the pistil in the centre (Chs. II, III).

Do you see that the corolla is made up of separate parts? Try, and you can pull them off one by one.

Each part or leaf of the corolla is called a *petal*. So now I shall be able to tell you about some of the easiest of the natural orders in which flowering plants are arranged.

CHAPTER IX.

CROSS-BEARERS AND BUTTERFLY PLANTS.

Fig. 30.—Bird's-foot Trefoil. (*Lotus corniculatus.*) *a* Flower.

We will begin to learn about a few of the easiest of the "natural orders" by looking for a flower which has its petals in the shape of a *cross*. The petals are four in number, and equal in size, and so they form a cross with four equal arms. There are several little plants with small white flowers which are cross-shaped, and which are common by the roadside or in waste ground. One of the most common has its seeds in a little pouch, or bag, somewhat heart-shaped, so it is called *Shepherd's purse*. Though small, its flowers are a good example of these cross-shaped ones that we are looking for.

Can you see any yellow flowers in the corn-fields that we pass? There are sometimes many of them, and they look very pretty just above the blades of the green corn. But they are very troublesome to farmers, and in some parts of England the village children are employed to pull them up.

These charlock flowers show the *cross-shape* very well. So does the wallflower—not the double, but the single one. Perhaps you have not seen it growing wild, but you know it in our gardens very well. By its side you can often see another example in the single stock, and you would see others in the flowers of the cabbage, cauliflower, radish, or common mustard.

Plants with this kind of cross-shaped flower are all put together in one natural order, the natural order of the *cross-bearers*. There are plenty of them to be found; and though you may not find many of them which you know, as yet, by their names, you will not have any difficulty, I think, in knowing them by their *flowers* (Fig. 31).

Fig. 31.—Flower of one of the Cross-bearers.

Of the second natural order that I shall tell you about, the sweet pea is perhaps the best example for you to look at. You may have some in the garden at home, and you very likely know what the flower is like quite well. But in a grass field, or by the roadside, we are almost sure to find a little plant which has flowers, smaller indeed than those of the sweet pea, and different in colour, but like them in shape.

Do you remember what compound leaves are? (p 22). Look for a little plant with compound leaves, like clover leaves, and bright yellow flowers. They grow in little heads or clusters, on some plants from three to five or six of them together on one stalk. (*cf.* Fig. 30). As in the sweet pea, the flower has five petals. The one at the top you see is the largest, and spread open like a flag, and so it is called the *standard;* the two at the sides are smaller, and are called the *wings;* then the two lowest are joined together, except just at one end, and are like the keel or sharp ridge along the bottom of a boat, so those two leaves are called the *keel.* So you see it is a flower with petals of such peculiar and different shapes as to be called after things they are fancied to be like—*standard, wings,* and *keel* (Fig. 32).

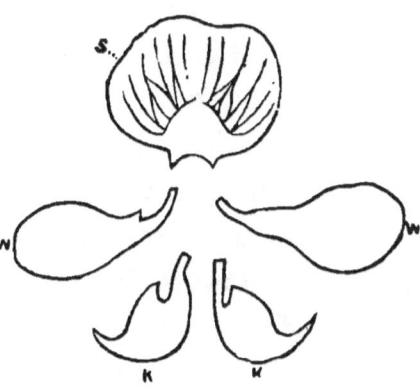

Fig. 32.—Papilionaceous flower. *s* standard. *w* wings. *k* keel.

But what do you think all the petals together have been fancied to be like? Perhaps you would notice it better in a larger flower, like that of the sweet pea; but all flowers with corollas of this shape have been fancied to be like *butterflies* (*cf.* Fig. 30 *a*, and 15 *b*). So the plants which bear them are all put together in one natural order—the natural order of the butterfly plants.

It is worth while to take one of these flowers and pull off the standard and the wings, then open the *keel*, and inside it you will find the *stamens*, ten of them, nine joined together and one free (Fig. 15 *c*). I should tell you that in some plants of this order the *stamens* are all joined together, and in some few the petals of the keel are not joined at all.

A common plant that belongs to the *butterfly* plants is the *clover*. We will gather one or two of the flowers when we see them—either white or red clover will do—and notice how the *standard* in these flowers is bent forward on each side, instead of being spread open. But these corollas of the clover are small. If we could find any of the prickly gorse or furze, we should see a better example of the *butterfly* corolla. Its yellow flowers are large and handsome.

One of the greatest botanists, named Linnæus, a Swede, when he was on a visit to England, and saw a quantity of it in flower as he was crossing Putney Heath, fell on his knees and thanked God for making anything so beautiful.

CHAPTER X.

LIPPED PLANTS AND UMBEL-BEARERS.

Fig 33.—Dead Nettle (*Lamium*).

I WONDER if you know the red or white *dead nettle*. Its stem is square, and its leaves are in pairs opposite to one another. Both stem and leaves are something like those of the stinging nettle, especially in the white one, which is the largest of the two, and grows about a foot high.

Both are common, and we shall very likely see some of them by the road or hedge side. You need not be afraid to pick them: they do not sting; and that is why they are called *dead* nettles.

I always think the white dead nettles are very beautiful. Their soft white corollas are large, and arranged upon the stem in handsome rings.

But look especially at the shape of the corolla. It is something like an open mouth. There are the two lips, and see how prettily the four blackish stamens are arranged under the upper lip which arches over them. There the two lips of the corolla join and form a tube, so that you look through its open mouth into its throat.

Take hold of the corolla, and pull it. It easily comes away from the plant, and you can see that it is all of one piece or petal. Now look into the little green cup or calyx out of which you have taken the corolla. You will see there four little things which look like seeds. They are really the four little bags or seed vessels of the pistil, about which I have already told you (p. 10). They will ripen into the four little nuts or fruit of the plant, and in each will be one seed.

The dead nettle is an example of another of those *natural orders* in which plants are arranged, and about which I am now teaching you.

All plants with square stems, opposite leaves, fruit of four nuts, and flower of one petal, with two lips, are placed together, and belong to the natural order of the *lipped* plants.

Their corollas differ a good deal in the length of the tube or throat, and in the size and shape of the lips; and I dare say we shall find some other specimens of this natural

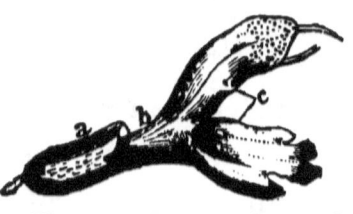

Fig. 34.—Flower of one of the Lipped Plants.

order of lipped plants as we go along. Though you may not know their names, you will, I think, be able to tell which they are. (Figs. 33, 34.)

There are plants, indeed, with two-lipped flowers which do not belong to this two-lipped order; but either their stems are not square, or their leaves are not opposite, or their fruit is not of four nuts.

If you remember the dead nettle and its four special marks as to stem, and leaves, and corolla, and fruit, you will not go wrong. You will always be able to tell a plant which belongs to the natural order of the lipped plants.

I must now help you to know the plants which belong to another natural order—the last which I shall tell you about at present.

Have you ever noticed the inside of an open umbrella? You can see several straight rods. They go from the little metal ring which is round the stick, and support the curved rods upon which is stretched the covering of the umbrella.

So in some plants, flower stalks branch off from one point like those straight rods do from the stick of an open umbrella. These flower stalks are not always equal in length, but generally nearly so; and so is formed a head of flowers, which is both round and flat, or nearly so. Such an arrangement is called a *Simple Umbel*. But from each of these flower stalks others often branch off again in the same way, and so is formed a *Compound Umbel*. (Figs. 35, 36.)

Fig. 35.—A Compound Umbel.

I am afraid I cannot tell you an umbel-bearing plant which you know by name, unless perhaps you have some little rabbits and so have gathered *kecksies* for them. These flowers are also called cow-parsley.

Many of the common garden plants, however, are umbel-bearers, such as parsley, parsnip, carrot, fennel, and celery; and these also grow wild.

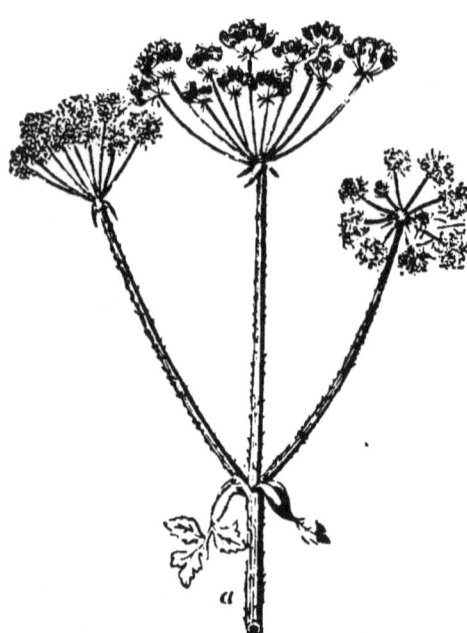

Fig. 36.—Part of stem of an Umbel Bearer. Cow Parsnip. (*Heracleum sphondylium*).

But we will look about to see if there are any plants with umbels of small white or whitish flowers at all like what I have been telling you about. They are common almost everywhere, and you will not have any difficulty, I think, in finding some of them.

If we pass through a wood, or any grass-fields, there is one umbel-bearer you may find which you can easily tell by its stem. It is a small plant, about half a foot or a foot high. It is easily pulled up. Then if you look at the lower part of the stem you will see that it is white and shiny, and waved.

If you were to dig down carefully to the bottom of the stem you would find there a little brown ball, of which pigs are said to be fond, and that is why the plant is called the earth or pig nut.

As some plants have flowers which at first sight you may think are of this natural order of umbel-bearers, be careful to examine them. All umbel-bearers of this natural order have five petals, five stamens, and you can see two separate ends at the top of the pistil.

As we go home you shall see how many different examples you can find of the four natural orders you have learnt about. They are the *cross-bearers*, the *butterfly plants*, the *lipped plants*, and the *umbel-bearers*. With a little practice you will know them quite well.

CHAPTER XI.

GENUS AND SPECIES.

Fig. 37.—The Daisy (*Bellis perennis.*)

WE will begin to-day by looking for some of the *butterfly* plants. We shall soon find the little yellow *Bird's Foot Trefoil*, which, I hope you now know quite well. (Fig. 30). There is generally some of it by the roadside or in a grass-field. Pick a few of the flowers, and also some of the red or white clover: they too are common. Compare now the bird's foot trefoil and the clover. Although they are both *butterfly* plants, and so belong, as you know, to one *natural order*, yet there is a good deal of difference between them. The furze, with its large soft yellow flowers and woody branches, sharp with spines, is another butterfly plant, but it shows a still greater difference. Because of these differences between plants of the same natural order, they are arranged in smaller divisions, each of which is called a *genus*. I am afraid this word *genus* sounds rather strange to you, but try and remember it. It will help you to do so, if you think of it as meaning a *family* division.

So in the natural order of butterfly plants you have the *furze* family, the *clover* family, and many others. In the same way, amongst the umbel-bearers there is the *carrot* family, the *earth-nut* family, and many more. In like manner all the natural orders are divided into families or *genera*, which is the plural of genus. Two of the commonest plants, the daisy and the dandelion will help you to remember this.

Take a daisy, pull off one of its white outside petals, and you will see something which looks soft and downy at the end of it. It is a pistil, and the white petal with its pistil is a flower, though not a perfect one. But look at the middle of the daisy. It is a bunch of yellow flowers. If they were magnified, their beautiful yellow corollas would remind you of the yellow crocus. Inside each of them you would see the stamens and pistil. So the daisy flower is made up of many little yellow flowers surrounded by little white ones. Each of them is without a green calyx and without a stalk, but all are set in the top of one common stalk and surrounded by some little green leaves which are very much like a calyx. This kind of flower is called a *composite* one, because it is composed or made up of many little flowers or *florets*. All plants which have these flowers are placed together in one natural order, the natural order of *composite* plants. (*cf* Fig. 37, *a* and *b*.)

But now take the dandelion. Each of its yellow petals has stamens and pistils, and in this case also the whole flower is *composed* or *made up* of many little flowers. So the dandelion and the daisy both belong to the natural order of the *composites*. But still they are clearly different from one another. The difference is such that they belong to different divisions of their natural order, each of which is called a *family* or *genus*.

So now I can tell you that every plant has a family name. We have our Browns, or Bulls, or Hunters, and amongst the plants there are the Buttercups, the Dead Nettles, the Clovers, the Daisies, and the Dandelions.

But you have another name, Mary or Kate, or John or Robert, perhaps, and by it *you* are known from the other members of your family. So every plant has another name, and for the same purpose. So we have the *red* clover and the *white* clover, the *sweet* violet and the *dog* violet, the *wild* cherry and the *bird* cherry, and so on.

This second name is called the *specific* name, because it is the one which specifies or marks a plant from differing plants of the same family.

All plants which are thus alike are called by one specific name and belong to the same species. So the plants in a natural order are arranged in divisions, each of which is called a *genus*; and the plants in a genus are arranged in divisions, each of which is called a *species*.

Our old friends the buttercups are a large family, and they will give us good examples of their different species. Let us go into the grassfield, and look for the tall buttercup, with smooth round stems and spreading calyx—the common meadow buttercup. Now, can we find one with the leaves of the calyx turned back against the stem and with its flower stalks furrowed? Loosen the earth round it, and get it up by the root, and see how it is swollen at the bottom of the stem. This is another species or member of the genus, and it is called the *bulbous* buttercup. (Fig. 2.) By the roadside, by walls, in shady places, we shall find still another specimen. Its stalks are furrowed, but its calyx is spreading, and it has *runners*, which creep along the ground and throw out roots. This is called the *creeping* buttercup. Every plant, then, has a *first* name to tell its family or genus, and a *second* name to tell the members of the family from one another.

CHAPTER XII.

USES OF PLANTS.

Fig. 38.—The Deadly Nightshade.
(*Atropa belladonna.*)

THE grass by the roadside reminds us how *useful* plants are to mankind for *food*, for no natural order is more so than that of the grasses. The wheat, the barley, and the oats of our cornfields all belong to it, and so does rice, which is the chief food of so many millions of people in the East. But if we begin to count up the plants we use for food, how many there are. You can easily tell me more than a dozen, the stems, or leaves, or seed vessels, or seeds of which we use as vegetables or as fruit, and there are very many more which you have never seen or heard of.

But some plants are very poisonous. Perhaps you have seen the bright red berries growing in the hedgebanks, or in the woods, in autumn—a cluster of them upon one short stalk. They are the fruit of "lords and ladies." But do not pick them. They may look nice, but several of our wild English fruits would do you great harm, and perhaps kill you, if you were to eat them. One of them, with a berry like a black cherry, is so poisonous that it is called the "deadly nightshade" (Fig. 38). Never eat any berries or other parts of plants unless you know that they are good for food.

But here is the dandelion, and we may take it as an instance of the use of plants in *medicine*. Not only do plants give us food that we may live and grow, but they give us medicine, to ease our pains, and make us well again when we have fallen ill. Rhubarb, and castor oil, and senna tea, what nasty things they are, and yet so useful to do us good. And so are very many of our common plants at home.

If you took one of the common stinging nettles, and beat its stem against a tree, or bruised it with a stick upon the ground, you would find how tough its stem is. It is stringy or fibrous. Many other plants are so, and from them are made several kinds of matting and linen. From other plants we get our cotton and many things which are used as *clothing*.

If oak trees are growing in the neighbourhood, we

may find some oak apples. They are called *galls*, and are caused first of all by a little fly, which makes a hole under the skin of the oak, where it lays its eggs. Some kinds of these galls are smaller, and quite round and hard. You often see them with a little round hole in them, which has been made by the grub of the fly when it ate its way out of the little cell where it was born. If we look at the wild rose bushes we may find something of the same kind there. They are a good size, and are covered with hairs which are often coloured red.

The galls of an oak which grows in Asia Minor are used for making ink. Have you ever seen, in the woods, great piles of oak bark? It is used for tanning leather; and there are oaks which grow in France and Spain, of which the bark supplies what we know as cork.

But the grasses, and the dandelion, and the nettle, and the oak have reminded us of the uses of plants, not only for food, or clothing, or medicine, but in very many other ways. This is a very important part of Botany, and you will find it full of interest.

You will notice also how different plants grow in different soils; and this kind of knowledge is useful to the gardener, the farmer, and the geologist.

A collection of dried plants is very useful to a Botanist, and, if you are fond of Botany, you will probably like to make one for yourself. In case you should do so, I shall add a few hints in a postscript to this short chapter.

I hope what I have written to you has helped you to spend some happy hours in "Flower-land," and to make a beginning of a knowledge of plants which shall be a pleasure and of use to you all your life long. As you notice and admire their beauty and usefulness more and more, I trust you will also grow in reverence and gratitude towards God, who is our Heavenly Father, and the great Creator and Preserver of all things.

TO MAKE A COLLECTION OF PLANTS.

Fig. 39.—Stonecrop (*Sedum*).

You will want a small tin to carry your specimens in. In the hand they would sooner begin to wither, and would be more easily crushed. Choose plants with at least two well-opened flowers, and with unbroken leaves, and take the plant with its root. Try to get specimens of bud and fruit as well as flower, and if you can find them all on one plant so much the better.

Root leaves are sometimes very different from stem leaves, and sometimes root leaves and calyx soon wither and fall off. Try to get examples of such differences as these, but if you cannot, make a note of them, so that when you have dried the plants and placed them in your collection you can write it down there. Note also the place where you found the plant, with the day of the month and year. You will often have to write a note describing the kind of root a plant has, as many of them are too thick to put in a collection.

When you get home you will dry your specimens between sheets of thickish paper, which will absorb their moisture. Then be careful how you lay them out. Turn one of the leaves so as to show the under side of it. Arrange the flowers so as to show as much of the petals, stamens, and pistil as you can, but turn one of them face downwards on the paper so as to show the calyx.

With these exceptions, place the plant on the paper as naturally as possible, so that you may keep before your eye its natural shape and manner of growth. Place plenty of paper between each plant, especially between those which have much sap in them. Do not put every plant in the centre of the sheet on which you dry it, but try and arrange so that when you have a pile of drying plants it may not bulge out in the middle, but be as level as possible. Then put boards above and below, and a good heavy weight on the top. You should look the plants through at least once a day, and change all paper that has become damp. When the plants are quite dry, you will place them upon sheets of rather thick paper (cartridge paper), and fasten them there with strips of thin gummed paper. Keep these sheets separate till thoroughly dry. They will then be ready for your "Herbarium."

I have given you so many hints, because, if you begin to collect at all, it is so much better for you to begin well, and take pains from the very first. You will soon be able to get some very good specimens when you have practised a little, so do not be disappointed if you find it rather difficult at first.

As you know more about plants, you will write under each plant its natural order, its genus, its species, and its name, with any notes you may think necessary. And then arrange them under their classes and sub-classes, with a corresponding index, so that you may easily find any plant you may wish to look at.

PART II.

CHAPTER XIII.

A GENERAL VIEW.

Fig. 40.—Honeysuckle. (*Lonicera.*)

You have already learnt something about the chief parts of Flowering Plants, and how they grow; and a little also about the way in which they are classified and named. But I think you will like to know that there are other interesting things for you to search into about them. So I will tell you the branches or departments into which the science of Botany is divided.

1. That which you have been learning most about, the outward forms of plants and their parts, is

called the *Morphology* * of Plants or Morphological Botany. What a long word you say! Well, you must look at the bottom of the page and read how the word is derived or made up and so learn what it means. If you understand what the word means you will more easily remember it. You should always notice the derivation and meaning of words whenever you can. It will help you very much. So then Morphology is that part of Botany which teaches about the outward "forms" of plants.

2. But now take a part of a plant, the stem for instance, of a buttercup or of a large garden lily, and break it across. You cannot very easily make out of what it is made up. Or try a leaf. Or break a branch off a tree, and try and find out about the different layers and substances of which it is composed. Try it with an elder branch, for instance, with its bark and wood and quantity of pith. This part of Botany is called the *Anatomy* † of Plants. To learn it thoroughly you will need a powerful magnifying glass or microscope,‡ but with the help of some pictures I think you will be able to understand the beginning of

---

* From the Greek "*morphe*," form, shape, and "*logos*," a word, speech, teaching.

† From the Greek "*ana*," up, and "*temno*," to cut, to cut up or to dissect. Also called "*Histology*," from the Greek "*histos*," a web or tissue, and "*logos*," word, speech, teaching.

‡ From the Greek "*mikros*," small, and "*skopeo*," I see. An instrument through which you can see small things made larger.

this interesting part of Botany. You will look forward to searching into it more thoroughly when you are older.

3. So also with the next department, as to how Plants live and grow, which is called the *Physiology** of plants.

4. *Systematic* Botany, or how plants are classified and named, you know more about. You remember, I hope, from Part I., about the Flowering and Flowerless plants (Ch. I.), and the further divisions of the Flower bearers into *Classes, Natural Orders, Genera,* and *Species* (Chs. VIII. to XI.).

Let us try, for instance, with a clover plant, either white or red.

Kingdom -	*Vegetable.*
Sub Kingdom -	*Flowering Plants.*
Class - -	*Net-veined (as to leaves).*
Natural Order -	*Butterfly Plants.*
Genus - -	*Clover.*
Species - -	*White or Red.*

But before we try to place and name plants, I am going to tell you more about their parts, and then you will be better able to understand the words by which the different plants are described in Systematic Botany.

There are three other branches or departments which I shall just mention.

---

* From the Greek "*phusis,*" nature, and "*logos.*" Teaching about the nature or natural life of plants.

5. *Geographical** Botany, which has to do with the different places and countries in which plants grow, owing to differences of soil and climate.

6. *Fossil* Botany, which is about the stony remains or traces of plants which are found upon or in the earth, and are called fossils.†

7. And last, a most important branch, the uses of plants, or *Economic* Botany (Ch. XII).

So you see what a splendid variety is before you in the study of Botany. You have gone out upon your terrace as it were, and seen your pleasure grounds, and fields, and gardens, as useful as they are enjoyable, laid out before you. Let us go down and begin to enjoy them. So I am going to tell you a little more about the Morphology, the Anatomy, the Physiology, and the Classification of the Flowering Plants.

And as we go, be sure that you are not disheartened by these long names. Have a good look at them, and they will be like strange but interesting gateways, through which you will enter into different departments of your property. Yours, for the country is before you, and if you be as graceful in character as the flowers are in form, and take care not to go where you will do harm, you will not find many who will refuse to let you search and enjoy almost as and where you will.

---

* From the Greek *gè* (*g* pronounced hard as in get) the earth, and *graphe*, writing.

† From the Latin *fossilis* ("*fodio*," I dig), dug up out of the earth.

MORPHOLOGY.

ORGANS OF NUTRITION.

CHAPTER XIV.

STEMS.

Fig. 41.—Sharp-flowered Rush. (*Juncus acutiflorus.*)

LET us dig up a plant of our old friend the meadow buttercup, with its smooth round stem and spreading calyx (p. 5). The stem, the root, and the leaves are called *Organs of Nutrition*,[*] because they are the parts by which plants live and grow. But the other chief parts, the flower and its fruit, are called *Organs of Reproduction*,[†] because they are the parts by which plants produce their seeds, from which grow up young plants; stem, and root, and leaves, and flower, and fruit, and seed again.

---

[*] From the Latin "*nutrio*" I nourish.
[†] From the Latin "*re*" again, and "*produco*" I produce.

I shall tell you first about the organs of nutrition, the Stem, and Root, and Leaves.

Now if we can go into a garden and dig up one of the plants which are just peeping above the ground in a row of peas or beans, it will be the best way of beginning our second talk about stems (*cf.* Ch. V).

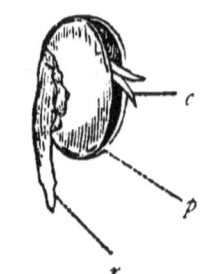

Fig. 42.—Bean beginning to germinate.

Dig up a plant carefully, root and all, and you will probably have the seed with it. You see that from one part of the seed the little stem has pushed its way upwards till it has just appeared above the surface of the soil (Figs. 42 and 43). It has come from a germ,* or young plant, which is called the *embryo*,† which was in the seed. Think of that. Snugly packed within the skin or covering of a seed is the baby plant. Of course it is very small, and its parts are not developed, but still it is there, and alive, that is ready to grow as soon as its circumstances are such that it can do so. Here is a picture

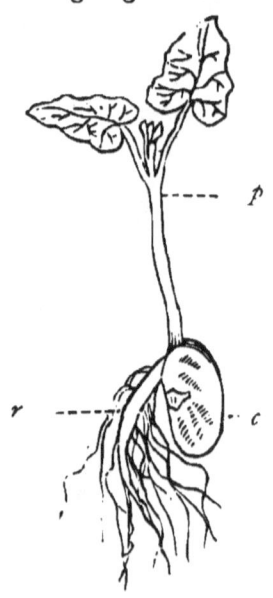

Fig. 43.—The same further advanced.

p plumule. *r* radicle. *c* seed leaves.

---

* Germ, origin. That from which anything springs.
† From the Greek "*en*," in, "*bruo*," to swell; the first beginning or origin of.

of it in the seed of the common broad bean (Fig. 48A). You are looking at the inside of one of the halves of it. Notice particularly the little thing like a bud at the point marked *kn*. It is called the "*plumule*," * and is a kind of stem bud or beginning, from which the stem in the plant you are looking at has grown up (Fig. 43 *p*). So it does also in all other flowering plants which are grown from seed.

If when you read this it is too early in the season to find a growing pea or bean in field or garden, perhaps you have some little mustard or radish plants just coming into sight—try one of those. Or if not, you will have a cornfield in your neighbourhood, with its beautiful green rows of corn just appearing above the ground. It is worth a walk to look at them. But when you get there you can easily dig up a plant, with the seed still there; and you can notice how the stem has grown out from one part of the seed where the plumule was. But now you know about the beginning of the growth of the stem or *ascending axis*. †

Now you should work through the following different kinds of stems.

Some are *scandent*.‡ These are climbing stems.

---

* From the Latin "*plumula*," a little feather.

† "Axis" is the straight line on which anything revolves, or may be supposed to revolve, from the Greek "*axōn*," an axle.

‡ From the Latin "*scando*," I climb; *cf.* stems of Vine, Hop, Virginia Creeper, Honeysuckle, Bryony, Convolvulus.

They climb either by the help of tendrils (p. 18), or by aerial roots (p. 75), or by twisting themselves round and round the object upon which they climb.

When the stem rises and then bends downwards to the ground, it is called *procumbent**; when the base of the stem lies along the ground, but the top part of the stem rises erect, it is called a *decumbent*† stem; whilst stems which grow altogether upon the ground are *prostrate* stems.‡ When a prostrate stem throws out roots and forms new plants along its course, it is called a *creeping* stem. (Fig. 14, p. 18.) Sometimes long slender stems are sent out which form small leaves at some distance from the parent plant (Fig. 44 *n*), and from these leaves, a new stem is sent on again. At these leaves roots also form and produce new plants. These long slender stems are called *Runners* or *Stolons*.

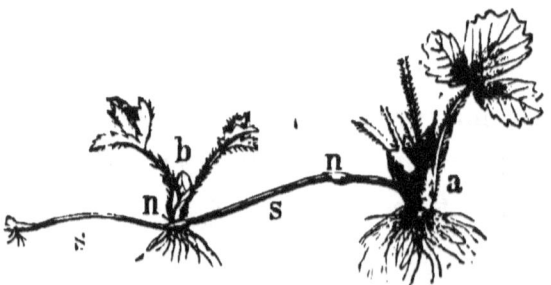

Fig. 44.—Runner of the Strawberry (*Fragaria*). *a* the parent plant, *n* the small leaves, *b* a new plant, *s* the stolon or runner.

Some plants

---

* From the Latin "*procumbo*," to lie down flat, to bend towards.
† From the Latin "*decumbo*," to lie down.
‡ From the Latin "*prosterno*," to strike down, to lay flat.

‖ Called a *Soboles* (from the Latin), a shoot or young branch. Some writers have used this word of lengthened Rhizomes, which you will read about further on.

die down every year to a short upright stem-base just at the top of the root. This kind of *stock* or *stem-base* has been called a *crown* because it is upon the root like the crown is upon the king's head. These stocks, however, vary a good deal in character as you will find when you compare those which I have mentioned ; and sometimes they remain visible above the surface of the ground.*

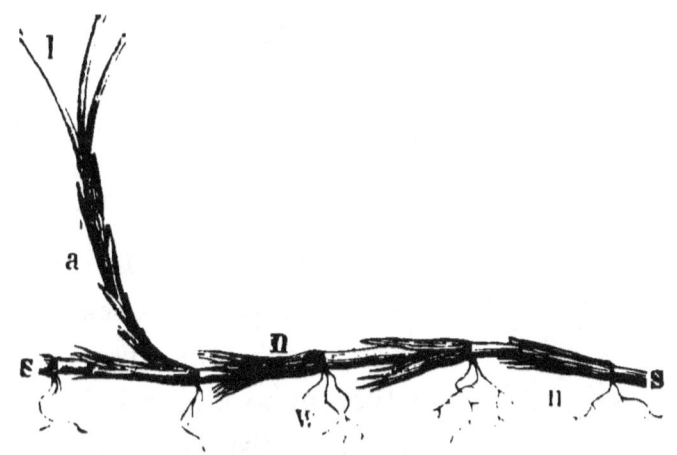

Fig. 45.—Lengthened rhizome of sand sedge (*Carex arenaria*). *n* Scaly leaves, *w* roots, *a* erect shoot with foliage leaves.

There are some stem bases or stocks which grow along (horizontally) partly or altogether under ground, and send up new leaves and flowers every year. They are called *Rhizomes*.† Sometimes they are thick and fleshy ; sometimes they are very much

---

*cf. Buttercup, Phlox, Rhubarb, Seakale, Asparagus, Horse Radish, Dahlia, Chrysanthemum, Fuchsia, Raspberry, Lavender. And *cf*. *Collar* in Appendix.

† From the Greek "*rizòma*," a root, a stem.

lengthened out and are comparatively thin.* (Fig. 45, cf. Figs. 1, 41.)

Search for these examples and compare them together ; pull up also and compare a common nettle. Get the plant well up so as to see how the young nettles are beginning to grow. If you search where the dead stalks of last year's nettles are, at any time from January to March, you can see this very well.

Then another kind of stem-base you know already. I mean a *bulb*, as that of the hyacinth or snowdrop (p. 17). The bulb is made up of layers which can be pulled off one by one. In some, each layer circles round the one next inside it. These are *tunicated* or coated bulbs.† (Fig. 46.) In others it is made up of plates or scales, which overlap each other like the slates or tiles upon a rounded roof, and these are distinguished as *scaly* bulbs (Garden Lily).

But I have not yet told you about what is called a "*corm*."‡ Like the bulb it is fleshy, but when you examine and compare them with one another you will soon see the

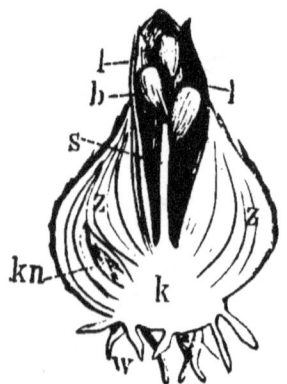

Fig. 46.—Bulb of a Hyacinth. *z* The layers or coats.

---

*cf. Primrose, Sweet Flag, Iris, Solomon's Seal, Wood Anemone, Lily of Valley, Sand Sedge, Couch Grass, Bindweed. cf p. 66, note ||.

† cf. Onion, Snowdrop, Tulip, Hyacinth.

‡ From the Greek "*kormos*," the trunk of a tree with the boughs lopped off, a log.

difference. The corm is one solid mass all through. If you cut it, it will be like cutting through a potato. The best plan will be to do so. If you can get the corm of a crocus and the bulb of a snowdrop and cut them across, you will not easily forget the difference between them. But the corm is sometimes spoken of as a solid bulb.[*]

Somewhat of the same nature is a *tuber*.[†] It is a thick and fleshy mass or plant stock which produces a bud, or buds, from which grows the new plant, root downwards, and stem, leaves, and flowers upwards. If you can dig up carefully a potato plant in full growth, you will see underground stems with these swellings, or tubers, upon them very plainly. We commonly call them the potatoes. I dare say you have noticed the buds, or "eyes" as they are called, upon a potato tuber. If, in the spring, you look at one which has been kept for planting, you will see the buds sprouting, and stem, and leaves, and roots of the new potato plant beginning to appear.

---

[*] *cf.* Meadow Saffron (Fig. 13, p. 16), Gladiolus, Colchicum, Crocus.
[†] From the Latin "*tuber*," a bump, a swelling, a knob.

CHAPTER XV.

ROOTS.

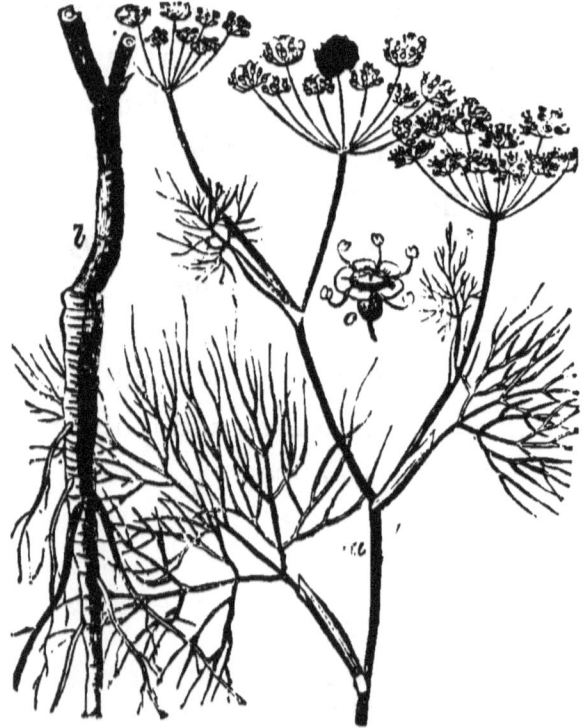

Fig. 47.—Fennel (*Fœniculum vulgare*). *b* root, *c* flower.

WE now come to the *root* or descending axis (p. 65), so we must not forget to take with us an old knife or trowel. As in our last talk about stems, so again we will begin with a seed which has just begun to grow. Search for one—wheat, or pea, or bean, or radish—as you did before.

But now notice that as the stem is growing

upwards, so the root is growing downwards. It has grown from another part of the germ (p. 64.) which is called the *radicle** or *root-bud* (Figs. 42, 43 *r*, and 48*w*).

Now let us see if we can find the common dandelion. If we can, we will dig it up with its root. Have you broken it? At any rate you have enough of it to see that it grows in a main or chief root down into the earth; just the opposite to a main upright stem, growing upwards into the air. A root, which in its main or chief part thus descends, is called a *tap root*. You are familiar with it in the thick and fleshy roots of the carrot or turnip. You will remember the shape of a common carrot or long radish. A root of that shape is called *fusiform†* or *spindle-shaped*.

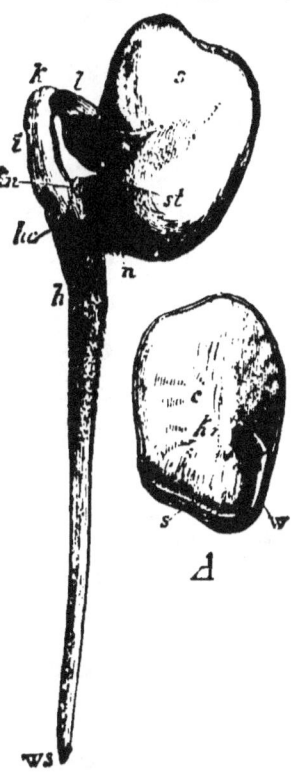

Fig. 48.—A Half a broad bean, B bean beginning to grow, *k n* the plumule, *w* the radicle.

The root of the turnip, you know, is rounder. Perhaps we may see some in the fields, and that shape is called *globose* or *napiform*; ‡ other words such as *conical, tapering*, etc., are used to distinguish

---

* From the Latin "*radix*," a root.

† From the Latin "*fusis*" a spindle, and "*forma*," form or shape.

‡ From the Latin "*napus*," turnip, and "*forma*," form or shape.

Fig. 49.—A fusiform root.

varieties of this kind of root. The hard and woody tap root of a tree is often much branched. And very often the main root of a plant begins to be branched so soon, and the whole root is branched so much, that you cannot clearly distinguish any tap root. Indeed, in some plants, the radicle does not grow downwards in one main root at all, but breaks out from the seed at once in many rootlets. You can see this very well in a young wheat plant whilst the seed is still attached to it. You will easily find one in this stage of growth if you look in the wheat field when the blades of wheat are just appearing above the ground. Now let us pull up a common plant, a buttercup, dead nettle, or bit of groundsel, and see how its root is branched. These branches of the root are called "*fibres*," and the root is "*fibrous*" (Figs. 1, 2, 27). These root fibres vary very much in thickness. They vary from the thread-like fibres of the common grass, to the string-like bluntish ones of the daisy or orchis; and to the thick, woody, cord-like fibres, branching and tapering down to fine and thread-like ends, as in the roots of trees (Fig. 50). The finest thread-like branches

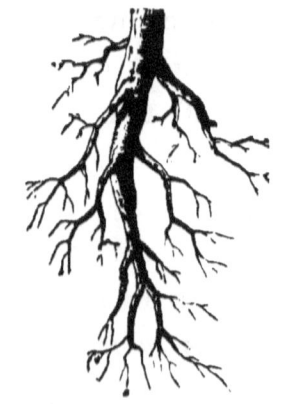

Fig. 50.—A branching root.

of fibres have been called *fibrils*, or little fibres, and if you looked at them through the microscope you would, in some cases, see upon them still finer threads or root hairs (*cf.* Fig. 29 *h*, p. 34).

As you look at these fibrous roots you can notice another difference between roots and stems. As roots are different from stems in not having any leaves (p. 16), so also they do not branch, like stems do in any regular order.

And there is another thing to notice. Sometimes a root has its fibres much enlarged into fleshy swellings or *tubercles* * as in the garden dahlia. Do not confound these tubercles or swollen root fibres with the tubers or swellings of underground stems. The tubercles do not break into bud as the tubers do. If you can get a gardener to show you some dahlia stocks when he is planting them in the spring time, you will see a good example of these tubercles, and then notice how the new shoots are coming from the old stem stock, and none from the tubercles alone. These tubercular roots are often called *nodulose, i.e.,* knotty.† When you know more plants by name you will be able to find such a root in the common dropwort (*Spiræa filipendula*), and to compare with it that of the water hemlock dropwort (*Œnanthe crocata*). In some plants these swellings are all along the root fibres, so that they look like strings of oval beads, ‡ and if you

---
* From the Latin " *tuberculus,*" " *tuber,*" swelling, bump.
† From the Latin " *nodus,*" a knot.
‡ That kind of root is called *moniliform*, from the Latin " *monile,*" a necklace.

can get a chemist to show you a piece of ipecacuanha root, you will see an example of a ringed or annulated * root. (Fig. 9, p. 12.) Do not be content with looking at the picture, but try and see a piece of the root itself.

But there are *adventitious roots* (p. 80). As for instance those which grow from the leaves or stems of plants. Perhaps you would not expect to find roots growing from leaves; but they do so in certain ferns. And you can find plenty that grow from stems. You will see them very well in the rhizomes, or underground stems of the bindweed, the couch grass; the wood anemone and others. (Figs. 41, 45). Compare also the roots from bulbs and corms (Fig. 13, p. 16), or of tubers, as those from a potato "eye"; or from the creeping stems which grow upon the ground, such as those of the creeping buttercup, wild thyme, and the ground ivy. (Fig. 14, p. 18.) This tendency of stems to produce roots, just as some roots have a tendency to send up stems, is seen very clearly when a gardener takes "cuttings" of plants or "layers" them. Parts of the

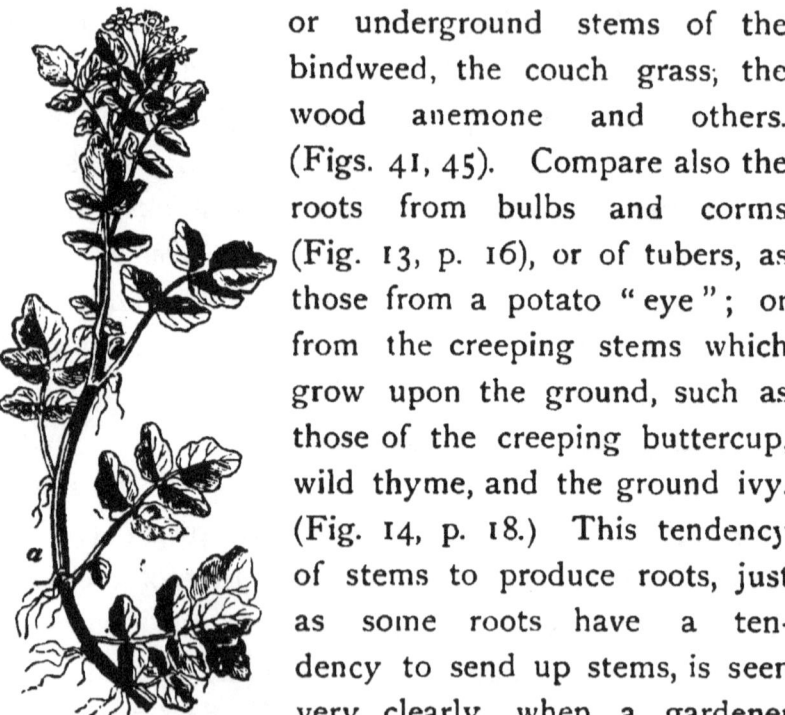

Fig. 51.—Part of stem of Watercress (*Nasturtium officinale*) producing roots.

---

* From the Latin " *annulus*," a ring.

stem thus planted or layered in the ground give off roots and grow into independent plants.

But sometimes roots grow from ascending stems, when they are called *Aerial Roots.* A familiar instance is the ivy, and you know how by these roots it clings to the trees or walls upon which it grows. No doubt we shall pass some as we go along. In the banyan tree, a native of India, these aerial roots are very remarkable. They grow downwards until they reach the earth, where they take root thick and strong, and a single tree thus makes quite a little wood of its own, and may spread over several acres of ground. All these are adventitious roots, and so also are those branch roots which grow upon old root fibres out of the ordinary course of growth.

As we go home I will just mention some plants which are called *Parasites* and *Saprophytes.* The former are called *Parasites,** because they feed upon other plants, sending down their roots into the plant upon which they live, and from it sucking up their food. A familiar example of a parasitic plant is the mistletoe. But some plants, instead of feeding upon other living plants in the same way which the parasites do, take up food from decaying matter, and these are called *Saprophytes.*† You will understand more about them when you know more about the physiology of plants.

---

* From the Greek "*para,*" beside, and "*sitos,*" food ; "*parasitos,*" eating at the table of another.
† From the Greek "*sapros,*" decayed, and "*phutos*" grown, growing (upon).

CHAPTER XVI.

BUDS AND BRANCHING.

Fig. 52.—The Birch (*Betula alba*).

Now can you find any buds? If you can, I want you to notice how different they are in shape upon the different trees. Some round and fat; some long and thin; some smooth and hard, as in the ash; some soft to touch like velvet, as in the palm and willow. It is worth while to pull a bud carefully to pieces. We will have one of the sycamore, if we can find it. Now peel off its scales, one by one, with your pocket knife; and at last you will come to a bundle of tiny leaves, very beautiful, and arranged in most beautiful order round the growing point in the middle of the bud. I hope you have a magnifying glass, and if you use it now, you will find how much it helps you. Now cut a bud down the middle, and from another cut off a good piece of the top. Let us examine in this way, one or two different kinds of buds: the larger ones, even if you have not got a magnifying glass.

If we can find a horse chestnut bud for instance, notwithstanding its stickiness, we will take off its scales. This woolly cluster contains the baby leaves. Open it out carefully, and you will see them, beautifully shaped, and wrapped up snug and warm in their woolly covering. Or try the buds of the common lilac. You will not search long without seeing the future flowers, in a most beautiful green bunch or cluster. Through the glass you can even see the shape of their petals. But perhaps it is too late in the season for us to search amongst the buds. If it is, remember that as buds are formed in the autumn this will be something to do on fine days in the winter and the early spring. How the future leaves and flowers can all be packed away like they are in the leaf and flower buds* is marvellous indeed. But

---

* Buds produce branches with leaves or flowers only, or with both.

though this is not more wonderful perhaps than the germ plant of the seeds, the contents of the bud are more beautiful to look at. You will find buds a splendid store for exploration during the winter months, and will enjoy searching out their wonderful and varied beauties, especially if you are fortunate enough to have a microscope.

If you pick a leafy branch of some common bush or tree late in the season and notice where the new buds are being formed, you will find them in what are called the *axils* * of the leaves. What are these axils? Pick any small leafy branch and hold it upright, but so that you can look down upon it. The crevice or angle into which you look between any one leaf and the stem immediately above it is the axil (Fig. 81, k), and it is in these leaf axils that all lateral † buds are formed.

But since leaves vary in the order of their position upon different kinds of trees, so also do the branches which grow out from their axils. And branches differ upon different trees, not only in their position and arrangement, but also in the manner in which they develop or lengthen out. For sometimes they grow almost erect, as in the Italian poplar; sometimes they grow out almost

---

* From the Latin "*axilla*," an armpit.

† From the Latin "*latus*," a side. Buds at the ends of branches or stems are called terminal, from the Latin "*terminus*," the end.

at right angles and make a spreading tree, as in the oak; sometimes they bend more downwards to the ground, as in the weeping ash or willow. Thus we have a great variety in the branching and outline of our trees (Fig. 52). Mark this as we walk along, and notice how greatly it adds to the beauty and the character of our scenery! There is a like variety on a smaller scale amongst the shrubs and herbs.

You will learn the different kinds of branching, and the names given to them, when you are more advanced. But you should learn now that branches generally grow in a regular order, according to their age. That is, those which are nearest to the growing end of the main stem, or axis, from which they spring, are generally the youngest. Their order in space is generally their order in age. And this order of growth is called *acropetal succession.**

But sometimes it is not so, for the buds may lie dormant,† and their branches are then said to be *deferred.*

And sometimes branches grow quite out of order. When a tree has been cut down, or its lower branches cut off, you can often see new stems shooting out from the base of the old stem. Such also are those stems which sometimes grow up from the roots, much to the annoyance of the farmer and the gardener. You may

---

* From the Greek "*akros,*" at the top; "*petalon,*" a leaf. Acropetal, growing, developing at the highest point of the stem or axis.

† From the Latin "*dormio,*" I sleep.

find them along the hedgerows on certain elm and poplar trees. If you can carefully dig up any of the suckers of a plum tree in a garden, you will see how they have sprung up from the roots. These stems are called *adventitious*,* because they grow out of order, and appear where they might not have been expected.

There is a little more which I must tell you about stems, before we pass on to leaves. For instance, what is the difference between a "thorn" and a "prickle"? Well, let us see if we can find a hawthorn,† or a sloe bush; and also a bramble, or a wild rose (Fig. 5, p. 8). Probably we can easily find a rose or bramble growing in a hedge of white thorn. Now we will take a spray of white or black thorn, and carefully take off the bark from one of its thorns, and from the part of the stem from which the thorn grows. Now try to break the thorn off from the stem. Now cut it off. You see that the thorn is a part of the wood of the stem. It is a kind of stunted sharpened branch. But now come to a branch of rose or bramble. You can break off the prickles easily. They are not modified branches, that is, they have not grown out from the wood of the stem like the thorns. You will understand more about this here-

---

* From the Latin " *advenio, adventitius*," that comes to, accidental, additional.

† From the Saxon " *hæg* " *hag*, a hedge. Hawthorn, or hedge-thorn; it is also called May-bush, or White-thorn. The Sloe has a darker coloured bark, and is therefore often called Black-thorn.

BUDS AND BRANCHING.

Fig. 53.—A thorny branch.

after. Now you can remember that *thorns* are the wood of the stem, whilst *prickles* are growths from the more external parts of the stem, and easily break off. Thorns too grow in a regular order like branches do; but prickles grow here and there irregularly.

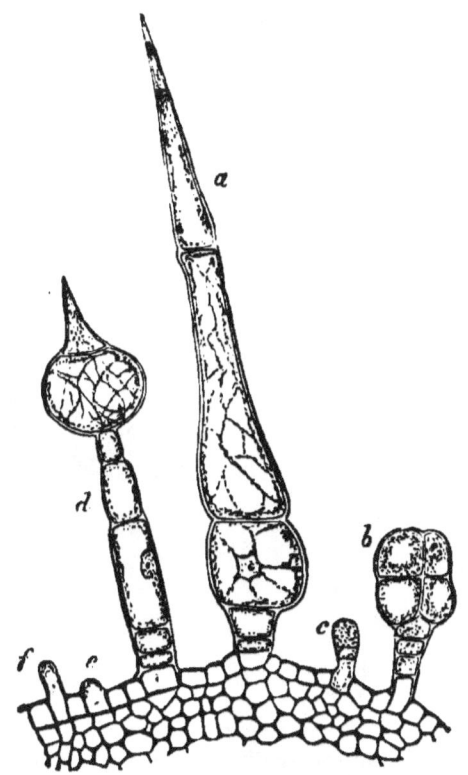

Fig. 54.—Hairs on young part of a plant (magnified 100 times). *b* Glandular hair, *c e f* early stages of growth.

Hairs grow from, and belong entirely to the skin of plants. They are found in many different forms—*clavate* * or club-shaped, *uncinate* * or hooked, capitate * or knobbed, etc. When they are stiff and sharp like a bristle, they are called *setæ*;

---

* From the Latin "*clava*," a club; "*uncus*," a hook; "*caput*," a head; "*seta*," a bristle.

and when they are enlarged at one end, swelling out and forming a kind of bag, they are called *glandular hairs.**

Hairs grow upon other parts of plants besides stems, and the surfaces upon which they grow are described by various terms, according to the character and quantity of the hairs which may be upon them. Many of these terms are words in common use, such as woolly, silky, etc. Some need a word of explanation, such as *pubescent*,† or downy; *setose*,† or bristly; *tomentose*,† or felted.

When a surface is smooth and free from hairs, it is said to be "*glabrous.*"‡

---

* From the Latin "*glandula,*" *glans*, acorn-like fruit, a soft swelling, or vessel more or less nut-shaped. *cf. Gland*, in Appendix.

† From the Latin "*pubesco*," to begin to have a beard; "*seta*," a bristle; and "*tomentum*," locks clipped off wool. Tomentose, short dense, matted hairs, making a surface like felt—on a woolly surface the matted, curled hairs are longer.

‡ From the Latin, "*glaber*," smooth, bald, bare.

CHAPTER XVII.

LEAVES.

Fig. 55.—Privet (*Ligustrum vulgare*). Showing decussate leaves. *b* The fruit.

Now let us see if we can find a dead nettle. We shall soon find one, either white or red, as we go along almost any country road. Notice the places where the leaves grow out from the stem. These places are called *nodes*.* In the dead

---

* From the Latin "*nodus*," a knot, a bond, a connection, a joint.

nettle the stem is thickened a good deal at the "nodes" (Fig. 33, p. 41).

It generally is so when several leaves grow out from the stem at the same level, and also when the leaves form a sheath round the stem, as in the pinks and carnations in our gardens. Or you can see these prominently thickened nodes in the stems of the common grass.* Now gather the stems of some herbaceous plants, and a few small branches of trees or shrubs, and point out the nodes to me as we walk along. Yes! any place where a leaf grows out from a stem is called a node. The parts of the stem between the nodes are called *internodes*.† (*cf.* Figs. 14, p. 18 and 44, 45, *n* the nodes.)

Leaves are always formed in acropetal succession (p. 79), and unless checked from any cause so they grow. So the youngest leaves upon a stem or branch are those which are nearest to its tip or growing point. Take for instance a simple unbranched stem like that of the dead nettle. As you go upwards from the base of the stem the leaves are younger as you go.

Now if you notice the position of the leaves upon the stems of the dead nettle, you will see that they do not grow here and there irregularly, but in a certain order. It is so upon other plants: and the different ways in which the leaves are arranged upon the different

---

* The stem of a grass is called "*a culm*," from the Latin "*culmus*," the stem or straw of corn.

† From the Latin "*inter*," between, and "*nodus*."

kinds of herbs and trees is called *phyllotaxis*.* When leaves grow two or more together at the same level of the stem, they are in *whorls* or *whorled* (Fig. 56). Now if you look again at the leaves upon a common dead nettle you will see that they are arranged in pairs, each pair consisting of two opposite leaves. Each pair grows so that its two leaves are over the spaces between the two leaves next below it. This arrangement of leaves is called *decussate*. † You can find examples of it in the privet (Fig. 55), honeysuckle, horse chestnut, and many others. You will learn more about Phyllotaxis or leaf arrangement when you are older.

Fig. 56.—Woodruff. (*Asperula odorata*). Showing leaves in whorls.

But before we leave the position of the leaves we

---

* From the Greek "*phullon*," a leaf, and "*taxis*," order, arrangement.

† From the Latin "*decusso*," I cut crosswise.

will notice what are called *radical** or *root leaves*. They are called so, not because they really grow from the root, but because at first sight they seem as though they did so. You know that they really grow from the stem base or underground stem as the case may be (p. 67, 73).

Compare for instance two common plants with radical or root leaves: the primrose in which they grow from the rhizome (*cf.* Fig. 1), and the dandelion in which they grow from its crown. (Fig. 138.) If you can find a plant of the common avens,† or herb bennet at the right stage of growth you will find upon it not only stem or *cauline*‡ leaves, as they are called, but stem base or radical leaves also.

Now let us pick a few common leaves—dandelion, rose, or ash tree will do very well; and hold one up towards the light, and look at the beautiful network which is made by its veins. (Fig. 27 p. 32.) This network or other pattern which the veins may make is called the *venation* of the leaf. I say this network or other pattern because sometimes the leaves are straight veined, instead of net veined. You will remember this from Part I. (p. 34). But pick a snowdrop or hyacinth leaf, or a blade of grass, and compare their venation once again with that of the ash, or rose, or dandelion leaf. Do you remember what I

---

* From the Latin "*radix*," a root.
† *Geum urbanum.*
‡ From the Latin " *caulis*," a stem.

told you about this difference in the venation of leaves? Quite right. As a general rule it is one of the marks of difference between two out of the three great classes into which flowering plants are divided (cf. Fig. 169).

But I want you to notice particularly two different kinds of venation amongst the net veined leaves. One kind is called *palmate.** Let us look for an ivy leaf. Now we shall see an example of this palmate

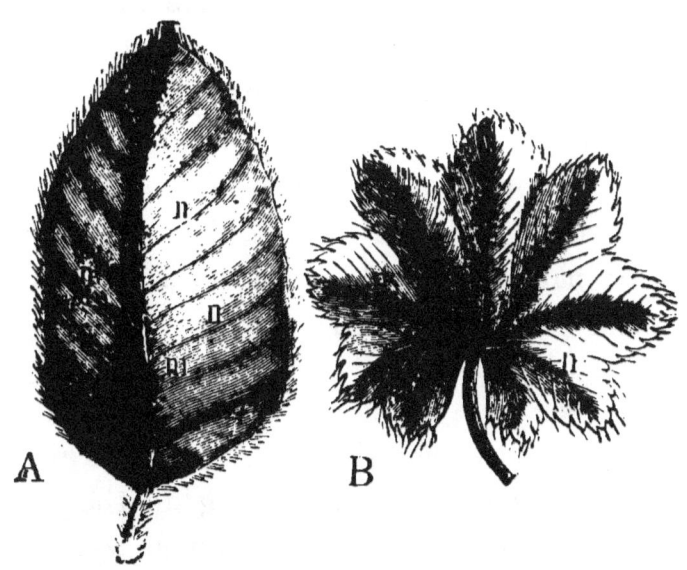

Fig. 57.—*B*, Leaf of Lady's Mantle (*Alchemilla vulgaris*). Showing *palmate* venation. *A*, Leaf of the Beech (*Fagus sylvatica*). Showing *pinnate* venation.

venation. You see that the veins separate into several main branches just at the point where they enter the broad flat part of the leaf. There is a very beautiful leaf in which you can see this kind of

---

* From the Latin "*palma*," the palm of the hand.

venation very well. Here is a picture of it (Fig. 57, *B*) ; but I want you to try and find it, for a picture, though it shows you its venation very well, does not give you at all a good idea of its beauty. It has been thought to be like a cloak or mantle, and the plant is called from this fancied resemblance of its leaves, the lady's mantle. It has small greenish clustered flowers. When you see the plant on a fine spring morning, with glittering drops of water on its beautiful green leaves, I think you will admire it very much. You will find other examples of this venation in the leaves of the maple, the sycamore, or the common currant. Leaves with the main veins thus spread out remind you somewhat of a hand with outspread fingers. This is why this kind of venation is said to be palmate, and the leaves in which it occurs are called palmate veined.

You will see quite a different pattern of venation in a leaf of the beech or elm (Fig. 57, A). Let us pick one. Here you see one main vein passing all the way up the middle of the leaf, and from which branch veins are given off on both sides. This is supposed to remind one of the shape and arrangement in a feather, with its mid rib and many feathery branches, so this kind of venation is called *pinnate*.*

Now we will pick a single leaf of the lesser

---

* From the Latin "*pinna*," a feather.

LEAVES. 89

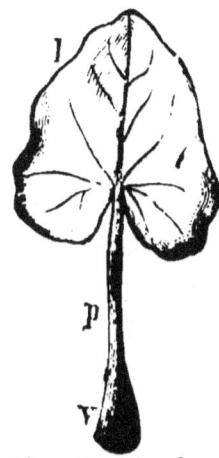

Fig. 58.—Leaf of Lesser Celandine (*Ranunculus ficaria*) *l* blade, *p* stalk, *v* sheath.

celandine if you can find one—violet, sycamore, or ivy will do—and I will tell you about its different parts. This broader part is called the *lamina** or *blade*, whilst the leaf *stalk* is called the *petiole*.† Take off a leaf carefully from the celandine, so as not to tear it, and you see that the stalk is widened at the lower end (Fig. 58). But now pick a tall leafy stem of one of the grasses. The blade, you see, begins at once from the stem. There is no petiole, as in the leaves we have been looking at. But if you look closely, and pull the blade of grass downwards from the stem, you will find that from the blade down to the node from which the leaf arises there is a portion which surrounds the stem (Fig. 59). Take a tall leafy stem of grass or corn, and pull the top part away from the bottom part. The top part will come off at one of the nodes, and you will pull it out from the leaf *sheath* of that node as you would draw a sword out of

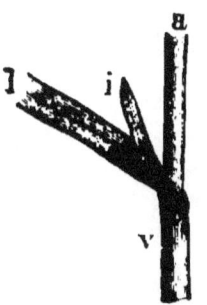

Fig. 59.—Part of a stem, with leaf of a Grass; *a* the stem, *l* the blade, *v* the sheath, *i* the ligule‡

---

* From the Latin "*lamina*," a plate or thin piece (of metal), a sword blade.

† From the Latin "*petiolus*" (from *pes*, a foot), a little foot or stalk.

‡ A ligule (from the Latin *ligula*) is a small tongue-like growth from the leaf, as in the picture, and common in grasses and petals of some flowers (Fig. 89).

its sheath, or an umbrella from its case. So that there are three chief parts of a leaf for you to remember—the lamina, or blade; the petiole, or stalk; and the sheath. Sometimes a leaf is not only without any petioles as in the grass, or without any sheath as in the ivy or violet, but it has neither petiole nor sheath. The blade arises immediately from the node, and so because it sits as it were upon the stem, such a leaf is described as *sessile* * (Fig. 56).

---

* From the Latin "*sessilis*," sitting (*sedeo*, I sit).

CHAPTER XVIII.

DIFFERENT FORMS OF LEAVES.

Fig. 60. — A Thistle (*Carduus*) with spiny leaves.

YOU have already learnt the difference between simple and compound leaves (p. 22), and we will take the simple leaves first. If the leaf is long and narrow, like a pin or needle, it is called *acicular*, from the Latin word *acicula*, a needle. If it is round like a penny, it is called *orbicular* or *circular*. There are many leaves which are between these two forms varying from the shape of the needle to that of the penny, and these are called *linear* (Figs. 13, p. 16; 174), *oblong*, *oval*, *elliptical*, and *rotundate*, or nearly round. as the case may be (Figs. 9, p. 12; 25, p. 28).

Then another set of simple leaf-forms is made up of those leaves which are broader at their base, with a more or less pointed end. These are called from various things to which they are like in shape; and

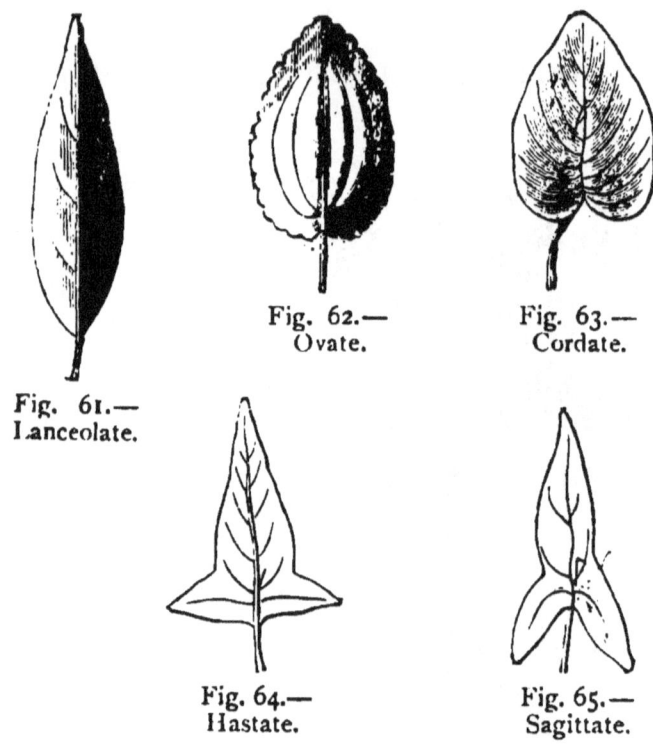

Fig. 61.—Lanceolate.
Fig. 62.—Ovate.
Fig. 63.—Cordate.
Fig. 64.—Hastate.
Fig. 65.—Sagittate.

are *subulate* or *awl-shaped*, *lanceolate* or *lance-shaped*, *ovate* or *egg-shaped*, *cordate* or *heart-shaped*, *hastate* or *halbert-shaped*,* *sagittate* or *arrow-shaped*, as the case may be. (Figs. 61 to 65).

---

* These words are derived from the Latin, "*subula*," an awl; "*ovum*," an egg; "*cor, cordis*," the heart; "*hasta*," a halbert; "*sagitta*," an arrow.

Sometimes they are just the opposite, the narrow part being at the base and the broad part at the tip. Then they are called *obovate, obcordate, oblanceolate,* or *spathulate,** which last you can see in Fig. 66.

Some simple leaves are called *reniform,** from their likeness in outline to a kidney. (Fig. 67).

Fig. 66.— Spathulate.

When the stalk does not join the blade or lamina (p. 89) at its margin, but at some part of its under surface within the margin, the leaf is called *peltate,** and these leaves are generally circular. You have an example of them in the pennywort,† so called because of its rounded leaves like pennies. These simple leaf forms are very various, and in describing them two words are often used together, as *ovate lanceolate* or *linear oblong.*

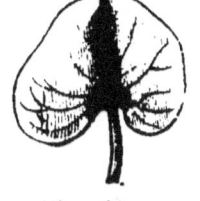

Fig. 67.— Reniform.

We will now notice the margins or edges of leaves. A leaf is

Entire—When its margin is neither fringed with hairs, nor interrupted by notches or indentations (Fig. 55, p. 83).

Emarginate—When its margin has a notch in it at the top or end of the blade.

---

* From the Latin "*spathula,*" a broad flat spoon or slice; "*ren, renis,*" a kidney; "*pelta,*" a shield or buckler.

† *Hydrocotyle vulgaris.*

Acute or obtuse—According as the end is pointed or the contrary (*cf.* Figs. 1, 9, p. 12; 38, p. 50).

Mucronate*—When, being more or less obtuse, it ends in a short, stiff, sharp projecting point (Fig. 30, p. 37).

Ciliate*—When it is fringed with hairs (Fig. 57A, p. 87).

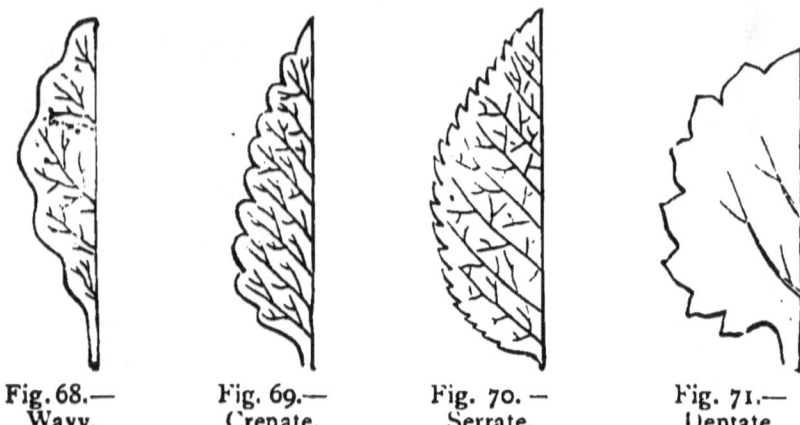

Fig. 68.—Wavy.   Fig. 69.—Crenate.   Fig. 70.—Serrate.   Fig. 71.—Dentate.

Then sometimes the margin is *wavy* or *sinuous* (Fig. 68, and Fig. 60, p. 91); but it is called

Crenate*—When it is notched in a rounded manner (Fig. 69).

Serrate*—When notched with sharp teeth sloping forwards, as in a saw (Fig. 70).

Dentate*—When the notches are upright (Fig. 71).

Sometimes the indentations of leaves are deeper, so that they not only affect the margin, but also the general shape of the leaf. When the portions between the indentations are rounded, they are called "*lobes*," and the leaf is "*lobed*"; but if they are more pointed

---

* From the Latin "*mucro*," a short point, a sword or dagger; "*cilium*," the edge of the eyelids, the hairs of the eyelids; "*crena*," a notch; "*serra*," a saw; "*dens, dentis*," a tooth.

and tooth-like, then the leaf is described by the use of the termination "*fid*,"* which means divided or cleft: for these leaves are described not only by the way in which they are indented or divided, but also by the character of their venation (p. 86). So if their venation is of the palmate kind they are *palmately lobed* or *palmatifid* (by some called simply *palmate* †), but if it is of the pinnate kind they are *pinnately lobed* or *pinnatifid*, as the case may be. (‡ *cf.* Figs. 57, p. 87 : 4, p. 7 ; 28, p. 33 ; 72, and Figs. 73, 74.)

Fig. 72.— Palmatifid.
Fig. 73.— Pinnatifid.
Fig. 74.—A deeply divided leaf.

There are two special forms which I must tell you of before we leave these divided simple leaves. In one form, the end or terminal *lobe* is the largest, and

---

* From the Latin "*findo*," I cut or cleave.

† From the Latin "*palmatus*" (fr. "*palmo*"), marked with the palm of the hand, resembling a hand with the fingers spread (*cf.* note p. 87).

‡ The terminations "*partite*" (from the Latin "*partio*", I divide), and "*sected*" (from the Latin "*seco*," I cut, cut asunder), are used to distinguish leaves with deeper and very deep indentations. Palmati or pinnati—partite : palmati or pinnati—sected (fig. 74). The term "*fid*" being used for those which are less deeply indented.

the side divisions are smaller as they are nearer the base. This form of leaf is called *lyrate.** (Fig. 75.) In the other, the end division is triangular, and the side *teeth* become smaller and have their points inclined towards the base: and this form of leaf is known as *runcinate.** (Fig. 76.)

Fig. 75.—Lyrate.

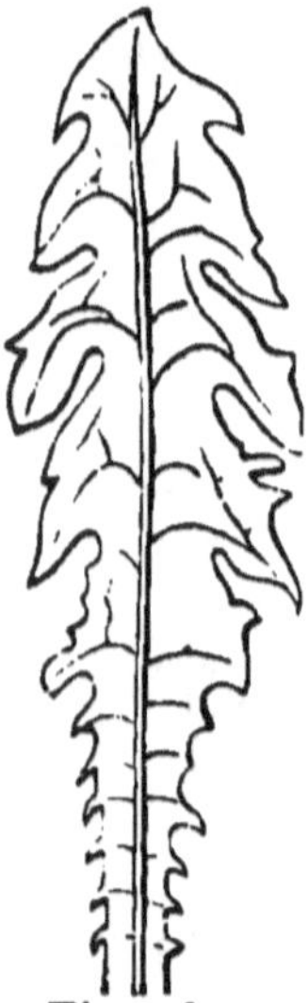

Now let us turn to compound leaves. These are either *palmately* or *pinnately* compound, according to the arrangement of their leaflets upon the palmate or the pinnate plan (p. 87). When the leaflets branch off from one point at the end of the petiole they are palmately compound (*cf.* Fig. 77); but when the leaflets branch off upon either side of the lengthened petiole, they are pinnately compound (Fig. 78).

Fig. 76.—Runcinate.

A. Palmately compound leaves are called *ternate* † (Fig. 30, p. 37) when the leaflets are three in number; and *bi* or *tri-ternate* ‡ when each leaflet is further divided into two or three leaflets, as the case may be. They are called *quadrinate* † if they have four leaflets, *quinate* † if they have five.

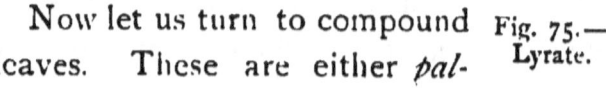
Fig. 77.—Digitate (Palmately compound).

---

* From the Latin "*lyra*," a harp; "*runcina*," a large saw.

† From the Latin "*terni*," three, leaflets by threes; in like manner "*quadrinate*" from "*quadrini*," four each; "*quinate*" from "*quini*," five each.

‡ From the Latin "*bis*," twice; "*tres*," three.

DIFFERENT FORMS OF LEAVES. 97

But when they have five or more leaflets they are commonly called *digitate* * or fingered (Fig. 77).

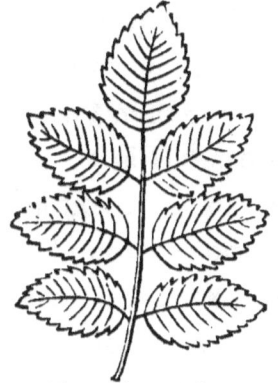

Fig. 78.—Pinnate (Pinnately compound).

B. Pinnately compound leaves. These are called *pinnate*, and their leaflets *pinnæ* (Fig. 78). They are *impari pinnate*, or *pari-pinnate* (unequally or equally pinnate) according as there is, or is not, an odd terminal leaflet (*cf.* Figs. 51, p. 74; 173). Sometimes the pinnate division is repeated, and the pinnæ are themselves pinnate. The leaves are then *bi-pinnate*, or *tri-pinnate*, according

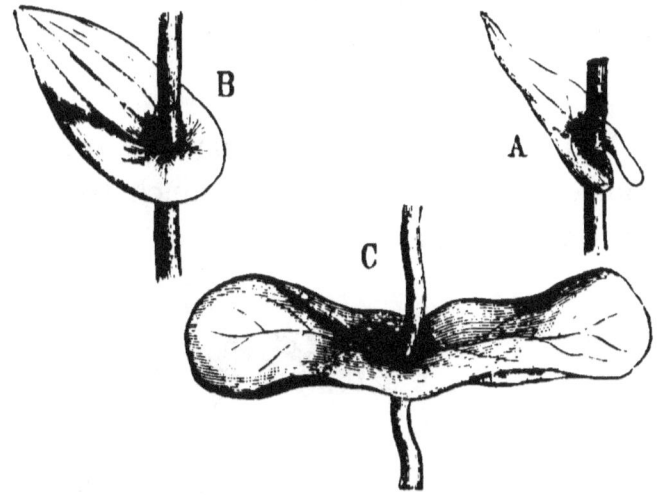

Fig. 79.—*A* amplexicaul, *B* perfoliate, *C* connate.

---

* From the Latin "*digitus*," a finger.

† When some of the pinnæ are larger than others, and the pinnæ are not arranged in order of size the leaf is *interruptedly* pinnate. Sometimes the terms bijugate, trijugate, etc., are used to denote the number of the pairs of pinnæ. From the Latin "*bis*," twice; "*tres*," three; and "*jugum*," a yoke, a pair.

8

as the pinnate division is repeated twice or thrice, and the leaflets of the pinnæ are *pinnules*.†

Now lastly, I must tell you that sessile (p. 90) leaves vary a good deal in the way in which they grow at their junction with the stem. They are *connate** when two opposite leaves are united at their bases (Fig 79, *C*); *perfoliate*† when the base grows out so as to extend upon the other side of the stem and surround it (Fig. 79, *B*); *amplexicaul*‡ when the extended base does not make the leaf perfoliate, but still more or less surrounds or embraces the stem (Fig. 79, *A*); *decurrent* § when the leaf extends down the sides of the stem on which it grows, as in Scotch and other thistles. And a stem which is thus leafy, or has a thin membrane projecting from it, is spoken of as "*winged*."

Care and perseverance in learning well these different forms of leaves will save you much trouble and delay in time to come.‖

---

* From the Latin "*con*," together, and "*natus*," grow, "*nascor*," I grow.

† From the Latin "*per*," through, "*folium*," a leaf; the stem passing through the leaf.

‡ From the Latin "*amplexor*," I embrace, and "*caulis*," a stem.

§ From the Lutin "*de*," down, and "*curro*," I run.

‖ For some other words used in describing leaves see Appendix B.

CHAPTER XIX.

STIPULES, BRACTS, AND SCALES.

Fig. 80.—The Carrot (*Daucus*), showing involucre.

But now I want to tell you about certain expansions which sometimes grow on each side at the bottom of the petiole, or stalk of a leaf. They are like small leaves or leaflets, but they are not always green in colour. Sometimes they are whitish or brown, and perhaps this is why they are called "*stipules.*"* They vary a good deal in shape, but are generally small, and from some plants they very soon fall off. Let us see if we can find some. The green stipules are easily seen upon willow, pea, bean, and the wild pansy. (Fig. 81.)

---

* From the Latin "*stipula*," straw, husk.

When two stipules grow up and round the stem so as to form a sheath above the junction of the leaves with the stem, you have what is called an "*ochrea.*"* You can see an example of it in the rhubarb, and in the polygonums. (Fig. 82.) Do not confuse this with amplexicaul leaves and sheathing bracts.

Fig. 81.—Leaf of a Willow (*Salix*). *k*, an axil bud; *s*, the stipules.

Now we pass on from stipules to *bracts.* These are leaves which are connected with the flower or with its stalk. They grow upon the flower-stalk or close under it, just at the point where it branches from the plant stem. If you can remember the leaf stalk and its stipules, so also remember the flower stalk and its bracts. You can see these leaf bracts upon the peduncles of the lime; as also upon the flower-stalk of the common colt's foot, one of our earliest spring flowers, and so called from a supposed resemblance of these bracts to the colt's foot. (Fig. 175.) Like the stipules, bracts are of other

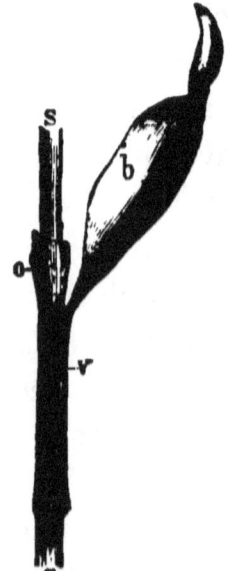

Fig. 82. — Portion of stem of Knotgrass (*Polygonum*), *b*, the leaf; *v*, its sheath; *o*, the ochrea.

---

* From the Latin "*ochrea,*" a boot, a greave.

colours as well as green, and they vary a good deal in form. I dare say you know the plant with strange looking purple or white things like long clubs each more or less enclosed in a large loose whitish kind of leaf. We used to call these plants "lords and ladies." Let us see if we can find some of them by the hedge side. If they are still young and not opened out we will unwrap one or two, and try to find the purple "lords" and the white "ladies." They are the flowers and I will tell you more about them presently. I want you to notice now the loose sheath in which they stand; it is a form of bract and is called a *spathe*.* You can see one of them very well in the picture of these lords and ladies in Fig. 153.

Sometimes these flower bracts are stiff and hard like scales. Here is a picture of one of the flowers out of the pussy cat or catkin of the common hazel. (Fig. 104A.) It has only stamens and they are with a scaly bract. In the same picture at B you can see some more scaly bracts which belong to those flowers of the hazel which have only a pistil and no stamens. About these flowers also I will tell you presently. Now notice only their scaly bracts.

But sometimes these scaly flower bracts have special names. For instance, look at the "flower of grass." If we can find one in flower a spike of wheat or barley

---

* From the Latin "*spatha*," a broad flat thin blade, the branch of a palm tree.

will do very well. Here you see the stamens and pistil of the flowers are enclosed by scaly bracts, which are called "*paleæ*."* At the bottom of the spike there are two bracts, in the axils of which no flowers are being developed; and such bracts in grasses are called "*glumes*."* Here is a larger picture of a spikelet of wheat which will help

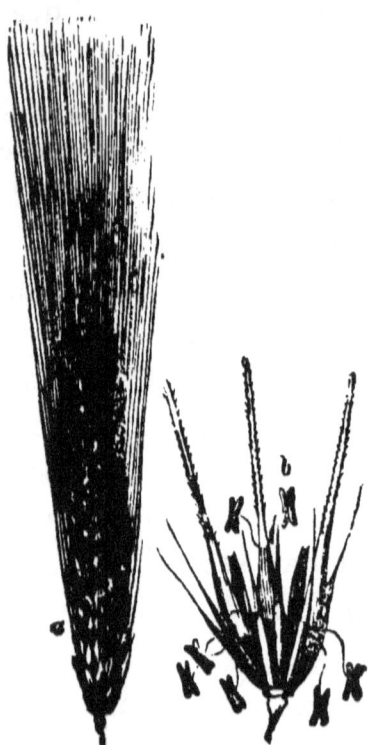

Fig. 83.—A spike of Barley. *b* spikelet.

you to understand this better (Fig. 84); and there is a picture of a flower of a common grass in Fig. 150, which you should turn to look at.

But let us pick an umbrella or umbelliferous

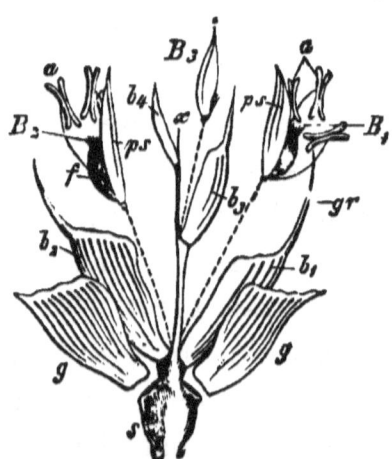

Fig. 84.—Spikelet of Wheat, dissected and magnified: *x* the axis of the spikelet, *g* the glumes, *b 1 b 2* lower paleæ with awn (*gr*), *B 1 B 2* flowers raised from the axis with the upper paleæ (*p s.*), *a* anthers, *f* pistil, with large seed bag.

---

* Some botanists call bracts nearest to, and enclosing the flower, "paleæ;" and the other bracts they call "glumes," the one growing opposite to the paleæ being a "flowering glume." The "*awn*" is the sharp needle-like point.

plant; anthriscus or cow-parsley, or any other we can see. Now look upon the flower stalk for a set of bracts, all growing at the same level of the stalk, just below the umbel. Such a ring of bracts is called an "*involucre*"* (Figs. 35, 36, 80, 86, 137).

Sometimes the involucre is composed of several rings of bracts close together, and arranged so that the bracts overlap one another, something like the slates upon the roof of a house. Let us look at such an involucre, for we can easily find it in some common composite (p. 48) plant. Yes! here you can see it very well in the dandelion, or in the thistle, or again in a common daisy (Figs. 138, 37, p. 46).

Is it too early in the season to find an acorn? In any case you know what an acorn is like very well. The acorn cup is an involucre made up of scaly bracts all joined together, and it is called a "*cupule.*" In the autumn you should look for the fruit of the hazel-nut (Fig. 103h), the oak (Fig. 114), the beech, the sweet chestnut, and the hornbeam, and compare their cupules. Commonly we call them "husks," but they are different forms of bracts which gradually develop, forming receptacles for the fruit, and botanically are called "cupules."†

Let us now turn homeward, and, as we go, I

---

* From the Latin "*in*," in, and "*volvo*," I wrap. Involucre, a barber's towel which he cases about one's shoulders when he trims one. " Involucrum," that which wraps or covers.

† Cupule, from the Latin "*cupa*" (*cupula*), a cup.

will tell you about some leaves which are still more different from the common green leaves than the stipules and bracts we have been speaking of. In colour they vary from shades of yellow and brown to grey and almost white; and being something like scales they are called leaf-scales, or simply *scales*. They grow upon underground stems, and are often very small (Figs. 44, 45, p. 66, 67). You can easily see them, however, in bulbs, both scaly bulbs like those of the lily and tunicated ones like those of the onion. If we pass any hyacinths, we will get one of the bulbs up, if we can, and look at it. The scales or coats of which these bulbs are composed, are modified leaves, or leaf-scales, and new bulbs often grow in the axils, just as branch buds are formed in the axils of the common foliage leaves (Fig. 85).

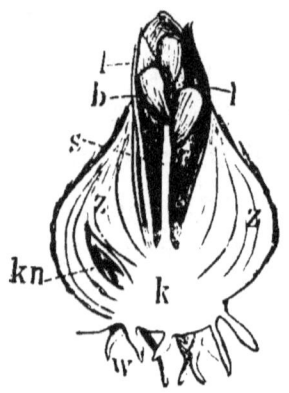

Fig. 85.—Hyacinth bulb. *k* Stem base, *w* roots, *z* scales, *kn* bud in axil of leaf scales which becomes next year's bulb, *s* flower stalk with buds *b*, *l* foliage leaves.

Sometimes leaf scales grow upon aerial stems, where they are most easily found upon the buds of trees. Do you remember them upon the chestnut, or the sycamore? (p. 77). The outer ones are smaller, but they gradually increase in size until the scale covers the whole length of the bud, then again they get smaller and softer, until at last you come to the tiny little cluster of delicate leaves, which I hope you have already seen.

You will find some buds without any scales at all, especially upon herbaceous plants, as you would do also in many trees in warmer countries, and such buds are called "naked" buds. But in most of our trees and shrubs the buds are covered with these leaf-scales, to protect them from the winter cold. What a snug little nest those delicate leaves of the sycamore bud were stowed away in, so that they were able to live on through the frost and cold of winter. And sometimes the scales have soft hairs upon them, as in many willow trees, and sometimes they are covered with a sticky substance, as we have seen in the horse-chestnut. These help to keep all that is inside so much the warmer. It is interesting to watch the bud as it develops in the spring-time, and then notice that the bud-scales generally fall off. Look at a horse-chestnut, lime, or sycamore bud during the month of May: you will see that the inner scales have grown larger as the bud has developed, some perhaps still upon the bases of the young shoots, but all soon to fall off, making quite a litter on the ground beneath. Those of the sycamore are beautifully tinged with pink.

For the rest of the way we will look again at a few of the common plants, and you shall tell me about the stipules and bracts, involucres and cupules, and show them to me as we go.

ORGANS OF REPRODUCTION.

CHAPTER XX.

FLOWERS—CALYX, CORROLLA, AND STAMENS.

Fig. 86.—Flowering Rush (*Butomus umbellatus*). Showing scape, involucral bracts, and linear leaves.

Now can you tell me what parts of a plant are called the organs of nutrition? Quite right. The stem, the root, and the leaves. They are the parts by which a plant is nourished, lives, and grows. We will pass on then to the organs of reproduction, the flower and fruit; those parts which have to do with the formation and protection of the seed, by which the plant is reproduced (p. 63). Can you tell me what the stem of a leaf is called? (p. 89). Just as the stem of a leaf has a special name to distinguish it from the stem of the plant, so also the stalk of a flower has a special name. It is called the *peduncle.** The stem (caulis) of a plant, the petiole of a leaf, the peduncle of a flower. But when the flower stalk is radical, that is, grows up from the stem base, with no leaves or only a few small bracts and bearing the flower or flowers at its upper end, it is called a *scape*.† (Fig. 86.)

Now look for a buttercup flower, and show me its different parts, telling me their names (Ch. II. and III.). Yes: and the top of the flower-stalk, from which these parts of the flower grow. It is often a good deal expanded or raised, and is called the *receptacle* or *torus*.‡ Gather a few flowers, and pull off their parts to see some different forms of the receptacle. There is a picture of the buttercup flower, with calyx, corolla, and stamens pulled off, in Fig. 176. (*cf.* Figs. 98 *t*, 100 *t*.)

But I will now tell you something more about these parts of a flower—the calyx, corolla, stamens, and pistil: and first about the corolla § and the calyx.‖ In the buttercup, you see, the corolla is made

---

* From the Latin "*pes*," a foot. If smaller flower stalks branch off from the peduncle or main flower stalk they are called "*pedicels*," from the Latin "*pediculus*," a little foot, stalk, or stem.

† From the Latin "*scapus*," the upright stalk, the shank of a candlestick, or shaft of a pillar.

‡ From the Latin "*torus*" a couch, cf. *thalamus* in the Appendix.

§ From the Latin "*corolla*," a little crown or garland.

‖ From the Latin "*calyx*"; from the Greek "*kalux, kalupto*," I cover.

up of several separate parts: you can pull them off one by one, without tearing them. You will remember that these separate parts or leaflets of a corolla are called *petals*.* So that a corolla which is made up of separate petals is called *polypetalous*.† You have already learnt about two particular kinds of polypetalous corollas: the "butterfly" flowers, which are called papilionaceous ‡ (Fig. 87 and *cf.* p. 39), and the cross bearers which are called "cruciferous."§ (Fig. 88.)

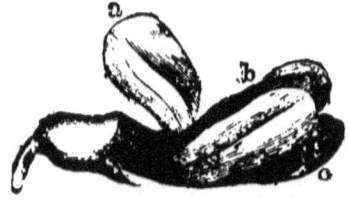

Fig. 87. Papilionaceous.

Fig. 88.—Cruciferous.

In describing the shape of a petal you would use any of the terms which would be useful, which you would use in describing the shape of a leaf (Ch. VI.). But I must also tell you that the broad expanded part of a petal is called the "*limb*," as distinguished from the narrower and more stalk-like portion which some petals have, and which is called the "*claw*." A petal of the common pink gives you a good example both of limb and claw (*cf.* Fig. 89.)

---

* From the Greek "*petalon*"; from "*petao*," I expand.

† From the Greek "*polus*," many, several; and "*petals*."

‡ From the Latin "*papilio*," a butterfly. There is another name for these plants. Their natural order is called "*Leguminosæ*," because their fruit is a *legume* (Ch. XXV.). This is the name for the whole natural order of which the British plants are "*papilionaceous*."

§ From the Latin "*crux*" (*crucis*), a cross; and "*fero*," I bear.

But can you find a primrose, or a red or white dead nettle? When you pull off the corolla from either of these you find that it is all joined together in one piece. And so this kind of corolla is called "*gamopetalous*." *

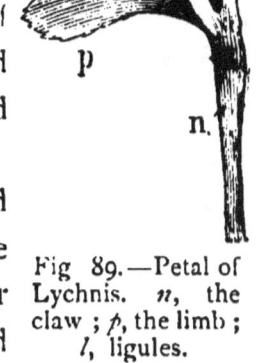

Fig 89.—Petal of Lychnis. *n*, the claw; *p*, the limb; *l*, ligules.

Fig. 90.—Gamopetalous corolla, showing limb and tube, salver shaped.

The upper expanded part is still called the "*limb*," but the lower narrowed part is called the "*tube*" (Fig. 90). Some of these gamopetalous corollas are called "*labiate*,"† or lipped (Fig. 91). If the lips are open, they are called *ringent* † or gaping, as in the dead nettle; if the lips are closed, as in the snap-dragon,

Fig. 91.—Labiate corolla, ringent.

Fig. 92.—Campanulate.

they are "*personate*."† Other words are used to describe gamopetalous corollas, such as *rotate*† or wheel-shaped, when the limb is spreading and the tube is short, compare speedwell (*Veronica*) and elder (*Sambucus*); *salver-shaped* if the tube is long, as in the lilac and the primrose; *campanulate*† or bell-shaped as in the

---

* From the Greek "*gamos*," marriage and petals.
† See note † on next page.

hair-bell * (*cf.* Fig. 92); and other words which are easy to understand, as *tubular*, in a single central flower of the daisy; or *funnel-shaped*, of which the common bindweed is a good example. In the dandelion you have an example of *ligulate*† or strap-shaped corollas (Fig. 138).

Let us look for some examples of the gamopetalous and polypetalous corollas as we go along.

But we must notice also the same difference with regard to the calyx. Can you find either the common creeping buttercup,‡ or the common upright meadow buttercup,§ with its smooth round stem? If you can you will see its calyx spreading out under the corolla; and you can pull off its separate parts or leaflets, without tearing them, just as you can do with the polypetalous corolla. These leaflets of the calyx are called *sepals*.‖ So sometimes a calyx is *polysepalous*, as in the buttercup (Fig. 93).

But sometimes you find it all in one piece, as in the primrose or the dead nettle, a calyx that is *gamosepalous* (Fig. 87).

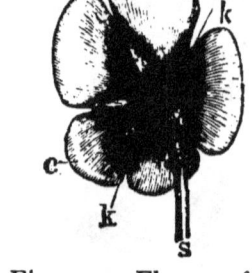

Fig. 93.—Flower of Buttercup (*Ranunculus acris*); *s* the peduncle, *c* polypetalous corolla, *k* polysepalous calyx.

---

* *Capanula rotundifolia*, hair-bell or hare-bell, common bell flower.

† From the Latin "*labium*," a lip; "*ringor*," I grin; "*persona*," a mask or false face; "*rota*," a wheel; "*campanula*," a bell; "*ligula*," a slip or tongue (of land).

‡ *Ranunculus repens*.

§ *Ranunculus acris*.

‖ From the Latin (*sepalum*) "*sepio*," I enclose.

The calyx and corolla are together called the *perianth* *; but the word is more particularly used to signify either calyx or corolla, when a flower has not got both but only one of them.

Sometimes, however, you find an extra calyx close under the first one. Such a second calyx is called a caliculus (little calyx) or epicalyx.† You can see it in the strawberry (*Fragaria*), or common cinquefoil ‡ (Fig. 94): and when you have an opportunity compare also the flowers of the common mallow, and the garden hepatica. These extra calyx leaves are considered to be sometimes stipules (p. 99) of the sepals, sometimes involucral bracts (p. 103).

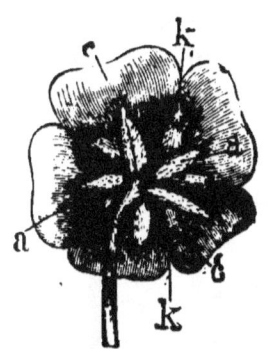

Fig. 94.—Flower of Potentilla. *c*, corolla; *k*, calyx; *a*, epicalyx.

Did you notice that I said calyx leaves? I said so because both calyx and corolla are really leaves: and so also are the stamens and the pistil. You must therefore add another to the kinds of leaves you have already learnt about. There are not only foliage leaves, and scale leaves, and bract leaves, but also flower or *floral* § leaves, those of the

---

* From the Greek "*peri*," around; and "*anthos*," a flower.

† From the Greek "*epi*," upon, and calyx.

‡ *Potentilla anserina*, silver weed or goose grass; *P. reptans*, creeping cinquefoil; *P. tormentilla*, tormentil; *P. fragariastrum* barren strawberry are all common.

§ From the Latin "*flos*" (*floris*), a flower.

calyx and corolla, the stamens and the pistil. If you remember this you will not think it so strange when you see a double flower in which the stamen leaves, or some of them, have grown more like the leaves of the corolla.

But now we can pass on to the stamens.* Gather a buttercup flower again, one that is newly opened, and place one or two of the stamens upon the palm of your hand. The dust bags of the stamens (p. 9) are made by the blades of the stamen leaves being folded or curled, and each dust bag is called an *anther;* † and the little stalk which supports it is called a *filament* ‡ (Fig. 95). The anther is very beautiful to look at under the microscope ; and there are not only different shapes and colours of anthers, but the different ways in which they open as they ripen, so as to let out the dust which is in them, are very wonderful. But more wonderful is the dust itself. It is called *pollen.* § It is not only wonderful in its different shapes and markings, although it is so small, but wonderful for its use. The pollen has a great deal to do

Fig. 95.—A Stamen. *a*, the anther ; *b*, the filament.

---

* From the Greek "*stēmon*," the warp in the upright loom ; from "*histemi*," I stand.

† From the Greek "*antheros*," flowering, because it belongs to the flower.

‡ From the Latin "*filum*," a thread.

§ From the Latin "*pollen*," fine flour, or the dust that flies in the mill.

with the formation of the seed, but I shall tell you something about that in a future chapter. You can see the pollen grains in the opened anthers in Fig. 109, *a p*.

CHAPTER XXI.

FLOWERS.—THE PISTIL.

Fig. 96.—Hyacinth, *c* showing ovules in trilocular ovary of its syncarpous pistil.

Now I am going to tell you something more about the *pistil.** Here is a picture of one, and you shall tell me what you know about it already (Fig. 97). Yes, it is made of a floral leaf (or leaves), which is so curled, or folded, as to form a bag, the upper end of the leaf being sometimes lengthened out above the bag, as in the picture, but it is not always so. Now, the floral leaf of a pistil is called a carpel-leaf or *carpel.*† The bag which it forms contains one or more little things which are

---

* From the Latin "*pistillum*," a pestle, to pound with in a mortar.

† From the Greek "*karpos*," fruit. So called because it is connected with the fruit, which you will learn more about presently.

called "*ovules*,"* or little eggs, and so it is called an *ovary*,* *i.e.*, an egg bag (Figs. 97 *c*, 96 *c*). We shall look for these ovules, and learn more about them presently. I must now tell you that the tip of the carpel is called the *stigma*.† (Fig. 97 *a*.) It is sometimes a simple point, or it may be knobbed or divided in various ways. Then sometimes, as in the picture, the stigma is removed to some distance from the ovary; the top of the carpel being more or less lengthened out into a kind of pillar. This lengthened out portion of the carpel is therefore called the *style*; ‡ and the carpel or pistil leaf has three parts, the ovary, and style, and stigma (Fig. 97).

Fig. 97.—Pistil. *c* ovary, *b* style, *a* stigma.

Sometimes, however, the carpel is not lengthened out; there is no style, but only the ovary and its stigma. You can see such a carpel or pistil leaf if you look at a buttercup flower, from which the calyx and corolla have faded away, and examine one of its separate pistil bags (p. 9). Each one is a carpel; consisting of an ovary and stigma, but without a style. § (Fig. 23, p. 27.)

But now I will tell you about the different kinds of pistils.

---

* From the Latin "*ovum*," an egg.
† From the Greek "*stigo*," I prick; *stigma*, a prick of a pointed instrument, generally a mark or spot.
‡ From the Greek "*stulos*," a pillar.
§ There are some few flowering plants in which the ovules are not enclosed in an ovary with a stigma. These plants are placed in a class by themselves, and you will learn more about them in due time.

First there is the *simple* pistil composed of a single carpel leaf. You can see one in the common pea or bean. If you look at one of their flowers you will easily see its single carpel, folded so as to form its single ovary: and you know it very well when it has ripened into fruit: the pod, either of the pea or bean. (Fig. 15 *d*, p. 21.) Then you can see the mid rib or vein of the carpel leaf very plainly along the back * or ridge of the pod: and it easily splits open both along the mid rib at the back, and also all along its under side where the edges of the folded carpel leaf had joined † to form the *ovary*, which has now become the pod. A pistil of this kind then, formed of a single carpel, is called a *simple* pistil. (Fig. 98.)

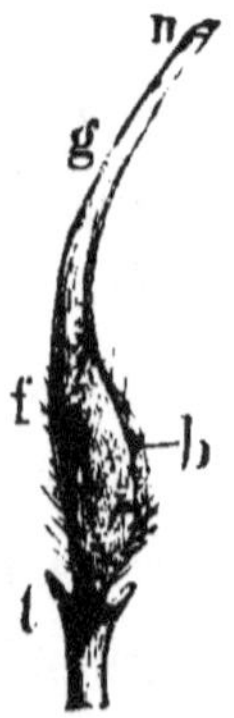

But very often the pistil is composed of more than one carpel. This is so, you remember in the buttercup. Look at it again (Fig. 23) and notice its many separate carpels, each formed into a separate ovary. So this kind of pistil is called an *apocarpous* ‡ pistil (*cf.* Fig. 99).

Fig. 98.— Simple pistil of Melilot. *t* torus, *f* ovary, *g* style, *n* stigma, *b* ventral suture.

But besides the simple pistil of the pea or bean, with its single ovary; and the apocarpous pistil as in the buttercup, with

---

* This is called the "*dorsal suture;*" from the Latin "*dorsum*," the back; and "*sutura*;" fr. "*suo*," I sew; a seam along the back.

† This is called the *ventral suture*, fr. the Latin "*venter*," the belly; and *sutura* as above. (*cf* Figs. 98*b*, 99).

‡ From the Greek "*apo*," apart from, and "*karpos*" (carpels); carpels forming separate ovaries.

its two or more separate ovaries; there is another kind of pistil. You have already seen it in the flower of the primrose. Do you remember it? We will find a primrose flower if we can, and look at its pistil as we did before, " the little round green bag and from it the slender knobbed stalk like a green and tender pin" (p. 10). This pistil, like that of the buttercup, is composed of two or more carpels; but they have so grown together as to form only one ovary. This kind of pistil is therefore called *syncarpous.** (*cf.* Fig. 100.) Perhaps you think the syncarpous pistil of the primrose looks as if it was composed of a single carpel leaf, and so would have called it a simple pistil like that of the pea. Well, but you would not say so if you were to cut off the style and stigma and look at the ovary through a good magnifying glass or low powered microscope; you would then see the joining of its carpels quite distinctly.

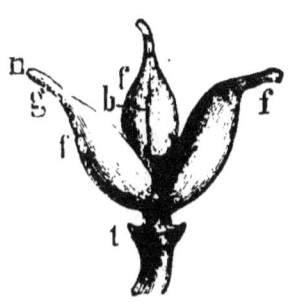

Fig. 99. — Apocarpous pistil of Monkshood (*Aconitum napellus*). *t, f, g, n, b.* as in Fig. 98.

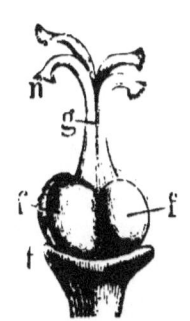

Fig. 100.—Syncarpous pistil of Buckthorn (*Rhamnus*). *f*, ovaries ; *t*, receptacle ; *g*, style ; *n*, stigma.

So then you have the three kinds of pistils : (1) the pistil of one carpel, which is called *simple ;* the pistil

---

* From the Greek "*sun,*" together, and "*karpos*" (carpels) : carpels together, forming one ovary.

of two or more carpels which is either (2) *apocarpous* or (3) *syncarpous.**

We must pass on to notice the position of the pistil and its ovary (or ovaries) with regard to the other parts of the flower. Sometimes it is at the highest part of the flower stalk, so that the calyx, corolla, and stamens are inserted upon the receptacle (p. 107) below the ovary. Then the ovary is said to be *superior*.†

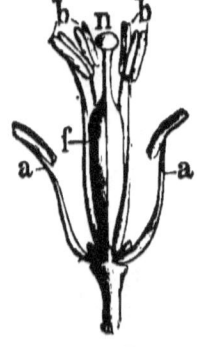

Fig. 101. — Flower of Brassica (corolla removed). *a* and *b*, stamens; *f*, superior ovary; *n*, stigma.

Once more we will pick a buttercup, and notice the position of the floral parts upon the peduncle. As you pull off calyx, corolla, and stamens you see very plainly that the ovaries are quite above them: they are "superior" (Fig. 23, p. 27, *cf.* Fig. 101.)

But sometimes the ovary is below them, when it is said to be *inferior*.† The tube of the calyx is often round the ovary in varying degrees; but you will learn more about the relative positions of the floral parts or whorls ‡ in one of the chapters on classification. It is sufficient at present for you to understand such plainly inferior ovaries as those of the willow herb, cow-parsnip, cucumber, or gooseberry, in contrast with the superior ovaries of the buttercup, brassica, wallflower, primrose, or tulip.

---

* *cf. Monomerous* in the Appendix.
† From the Latin "*superior*," higher; "*inferior*," lower.
‡ The floral parts being modified leaves, *cf.* p. 111.

But let us see what the ovaries are like inside. Sometimes they are simple boxes, or bags, without any partitions (Fig. 102, *A B*).

But sometimes they have partitions inside them to divide them into compartments, or "*loculi.*" So an ovary is "*unilocular*"* or *multilocular,** or more particularly, "*bilocular*,"* *trilocular*, etc.,

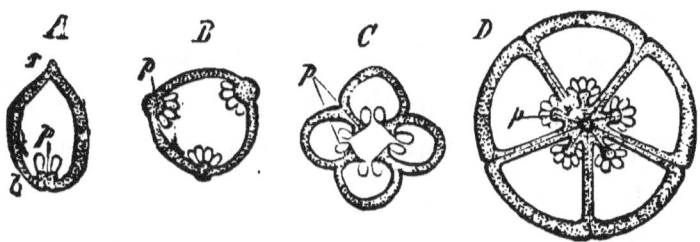

Fig. 102.—Ovaries with tops cut off (transverse sections). *A* unilocular, *b* ventral suture, *r* dorsal suture, *B* unilocular, *C* chambered (but unilocular), *D* multilocular (5-celled), *p*, the placenta.

according to the number of its compartments (Fig. 102 *D. cf. 96c*). Sometimes the partitions do not reach so as to divide the ovary into separate compartments, but only partly so. Such a unilocular ovary is described as *chambered* (Fig. 102 *C*, 123 *c*). These partitions are called *dissepiments*,† and are generally, but not always, made by the carpel leaves. You will know more about them in due time.

Now I want you to notice particularly the little eggs or ovules (p. 115) which are inside the ovaries. So let us look for a primrose, pea, or bean, or other flower that

---

* From the Latin "*unus*," one; "*multus*," many; "*bis*," two; "*tres*," three, and so on with the other numbers; and "*loculus*" (*locus*), a little place, a pocket.

† From the Latin "*dissepio*," I separate.

has a good sized pistil; and choose one that has just come into bloom. Now take off its calyx, corolla, and stamens; and when you have laid bare the pistil, cut open the ovary. You will now be able to see the ovule, or ovules, in it. That part within the ovary to which the ovules are attached is called the *placenta* * (Fig. 102 *p*), and the way in which the placentas are arranged is called *placentation*.*

But we will now look about for another flower with a large pistil, and this time choose one from which the corolla has faded away, or, as you would say, one which has gone to seed. And so it has. You cut open its ovary and see what once were ovules, but now are seeds (Fig. 108). I have a little more to tell you about flowers in general, and then I will tell you something about this change of ovules into seeds.

---

* From Latin "*placenta*," Greek "*plakous*," "*plax*," a flat cake, anything flat. See *placentation* in the Appendix.

CHAPTER XXII.

INCOMPLETE FLOWERS AND INFLORESCENCE.

Fig. 103.—Common Hazel (*Corylus avellana*). Monœcious. Showing stameniferous catkin, and pistiliferous flowers. *h*, the fruit.

Now I hope you know pretty well about the four chief parts of a flower, the calyx, corolla, stamens, and pistil.

But some flowers are *incomplete*. For you will remember, I think, that some flowers instead of having both calyx and corolla, have only one of them. Well, some have neither calyx nor corolla; no perianth at all.*

They vary also with regard to their stamens and pistil. You will not always find both stamens and pistil in the same flower. Can we find, for instance, the common hazel or nut bush? The long yellow catkins, which children call pussy cats' tails, and which I expect you know very well, are composed of *stameniferous* † flowers, that is, flowers which have only stamens. Shake them when they are ripe and you see quite a little cloud of their yellow pollen. In Fig. 104 A there is a picture of one of the flowers from one of these catkins of the hazel; you see that it has stamens only. You can see the whole catkin in Fig. 103. And now if you look carefully along the branches you will see some things like buds from which beautiful and delicate pink points are appearing. They are the tips of the pistils, of the *pistiliferous* ‡ flowers, projecting from the scales by which the flowers are surrounded. See Fig. 104 B C, and again, in Fig. 103 at the top of the branch marked *a*.

---

* cf. *monochlamydeous* in the Appendix.

† From the Latin "*fero*," I bear, and stamens.

‡ Flowers which have a pistil only, from Latin "*fero*," I bear, and pistil. cf. *hermaphrodite* in the Appendix.

INCOMPLETE FLOWERS. 123

But now compare also Fig. 153 *b*. *b* is the stalk bearing the flowers, the middle ring being stameniferous flowers, the lowest ring the pistiliferous flowers, the upper ring imperfect flowers. So the flowers of the hazel or of the arum (cuckoo pint) are called *monœcious*,* because whilst the stamens and pistil are in different flowers, both the stamen bearing flowers and the pistil bearing flowers, live as it were, in one house, that is upon one plant.

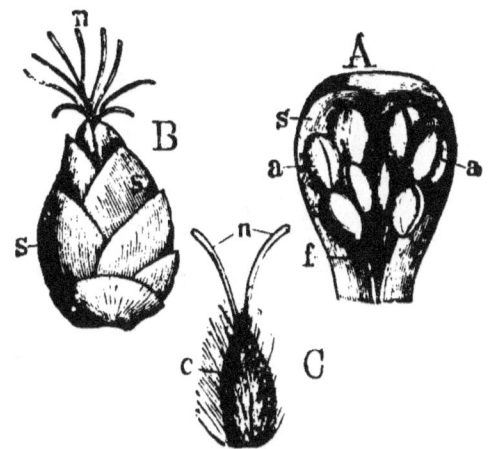

Fig. 104.—Flowers of Hazel; A, single flower from the stameniferous catkin; *s*, the scale; *fa*, the stamens; *f*, the filaments; *a*, the anthers; B, pistiliferous flowers enclosed in bract scales, *s*; with projecting tips of their pistils, *n*; C, single pistiliferous flower from B, surrounded by its bracts, *c*, with tips of pistil, *n* (magnified).

But sometimes they live as it were in two houses, that is upon different plants: then they are called *diœcious*.* We should have an instance of this if we could find the common yew tree in bloom (Fig. 174), or some willow trees, or the common hop (Fig. 105). But you very likely know the difference in the flowers upon the willow trees, several kinds of which are commonly called palms.† If you

---

* From the Greek "*monos*," one; "*dis*," twice, double; and "*oikion*," a house.

† The true Palm trees are foreigners. There is a picture of one in Fig. 134.

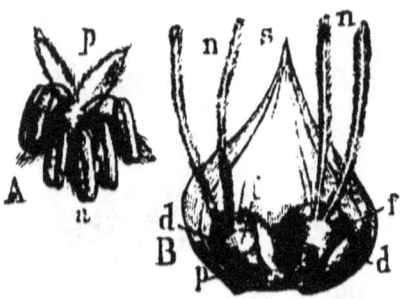

Fig. 105.—Flowers of the Hop (*Humulus lupulus*). A, stameniferous flower; *p*, perianth; *a*, stamens; B, pistiliferous flowers; *s*, stipule scale; *d*, bract; *p*, perianth; *f*, pistil bag with two long lips or ends (*n*).

have ever looked for these palms or willows for use upon Palm Sunday, you always like to find those with the stamen bearing flowers. Very fine are their full oval catkins, bright with their beautiful yellow stamens! but hardly less beautiful, I think, though not so imposing, are the trees with their pistil bearing flowers: smaller but bright and glossy as the finest silk.

Before we pass on to the formation of seed and fruit, I must tell you something about the "*inflorescence*";* that is, the way in which flowers are arranged upon their stalk or axis.

The inflorescence is called *a spike* when the flowers are sessile (or on very short pedicels) and are arranged more or less closely along the more or less lengthened floral axis (p. 65), as in the common plantains *(Plantago)*. This is called *a spadix* † when the axis is thick and fleshy, and generally with a spathe (p. 101), as in the common arum (Fig. 153).

---

* From the Latin "*in*," and "*floresco*" (*floreo*), I bloom.

† From the Greek "*spadix*," a palm branch; in which the spathe, which is generally with it, is well seen.

INCOMPLETE FLOWERS.   125

In the *catkin* or *amentum** the flowers have either stamens or pistil, not both in the same flower, and the whole falls off together when the stamens have withered or the fruit ripened, as in the willow *(Salix)* or the stameniferous catkins of the hazel *(Corylus)* (Fig. 103).

The *raceme*† has the flowers arranged along a more or less lengthened floral axis, as in the spike, but they have longer pedicels, all being of about the same length, as in barbery *(Berberis)*, foxglove *(Digitalis)*, currant (*cf*. Fig. 169).

The *corymb*† differs again from the spike and the raceme in having the lower pedicels longer than the upper ones, so that the flowers form a nearly level top.

The *panicle*‡ is a branched or compound raceme (Fig 106).

Notice, too, the spike of pistiliferous flowers, with hardening scales as it ripens into fruit and which you know very well as the *cone*, as on the pine or fir (Fig. 117) or common larch. And the *compound spike*, as in the

Fig. 106.—Panicle of common Oat.

---

* From the Latin "*amentum*," a thong or loop.
† From the Latin "*racemus*," or "*corymbus*," a bunch or cluster.
‡ From the Latin "*panicula*," the down upon reeds; a loose inflorescence.

wheat and barley, in which secondary spikes (spikelets) are arranged along the floral axis, instead of single flowers (*cf.* Fig. 83*b*. p. 102).

Fig. 107.—Compound umbel with umbellules.

The *umbel*,* both the simple umbel and the compound umbel with its umbellules or little umbels, you have already learnt about (p. 43). (Fig. 107.)

The *capitulum* † or head of flowers is composed of many sessile, or almost sessile flowers, placed close together upon the receptacle (p. 107) of the main stem, and the whole surrounded by an involucre (as in the teasel, Fig. 142). Sometimes the receptacle is hollowed out, sometimes it is raised and rounded. Compare them in the dandelion (Fig. 138), daisy (Fig. 37, p. 46), and other composite flowers (p. 48). Each flower is called a *floret :* those of the centre, as in the daisy, form the "*disk*," those of the circumference form the "*ray*."

The *cyme*.‡ Perhaps the best way to understand this kind of inflorescence will be to look at a plant in which the main axis or stem terminates in a flower. The common mouse-ear chickweed *(Cerastium)* will

---

* From the Latin "*umbella*," a little shadow, from "*umbra*," a shade, a shadow, whence also our word "umbrella."

† From the Latin "*caput*," a head.

‡ From the Latin "*cyma*," a shoot or branch, young sprouts.

do very well. Just below the peduncle, which is a continuation of the main stem of the plant, other flower-bearing stems branch off. Each of them ends again in a flower. But just below that terminal flower other stems branch off again, each bearing a flower and branching as before. Sometimes instead of two, there are three or more branches growing out under the main terminal flower. All inflorescences of this kind of growth are called *cymose*.

You will find compound and irregular inflorescences which will be best described as racemose, corymbose, panicled, umbellate, cymose, etc., according to the inflorescence which they most resemble. There are some which you will find puzzling to describe, but do not be discouraged, and as you become more practised and learn more about them your difficulties will gradually disappear.

CHAPTER XXIII.

FORMATION OF SEED.

Fig. 108.—Flower and fruit of Capsicum. *a*, fruit cut open lengthways (longitudinal section) showing seeds; *b*, the same cut across (transverse section).

WE will begin by looking for a plant in full bloom and picking one of its flowers. A primrose, garden lily, or some other flower in which we can easily see the pistil with its ovary, and style, and stigma. Is it not strange? The stigma and style have a channel or passage through them, something like there is through the stem of a piece of elder where the pith is; but sometimes the channel is quite hollow as in the stem of a tobacco pipe. This channel leads into the ovary just as that of a pipe stem does into the pipe bowl.

FORMATION OF SEED.

Now in due course some of the pollen grains of the stamen will be brought to the stigma of the pistil. There they will stick fast, being held by a kind of sticky fluid which is formed upon the stigma. Try if you can see through your magnifying glass any pollen grains upon any of the stigmas of the flowers which you have gathered. If not, look for a large flower that has begun to fade, and try again. In the little violet even you should see through a good glass the little mouth or opening of the channel down the stigma and perhaps also some pollen sticking round it. This settling of the pollen upon the stigma is called *pollination*.

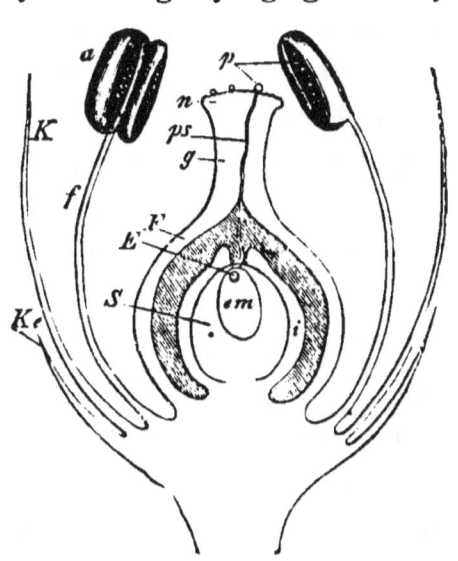

Fig. 109.—Diagram of a flower. *Kc*, calyx; *K*, corolla; *f*, filament; *a*, anther with pollen bags open showing pollen grains (*p*); *n*, the stigma; *g*, the style; *F*, the ovary; *i*, the inner covering of the ovule, *S*; *em*, inner bag containing the vital part of the ovule, at *E*.

But it is not always so good for a flower for pollination to take place by its own pollen as by that of another flower. Indeed this is sometimes necessary; for, as we have seen, the stamens and pistil are sometimes removed from one another by being in separate flowers (monæcious, p. 123), or in separate plants (diæcious, p. 123); and, in flowers in which stamens and pistil are together, you will often find that they cannot easily be pollenised by their own pollen.

Sometimes, for instance, the anthers and stigma ripen or mature at different times, so that the anthers may have ripened, and shed their pollen before the stigma of the pistil is ready to receive it; sometimes the anthers and stigma are so placed that the pollen of the flower cannot easily come in contact with it own stigma; and sometimes, if it does so, it is of no use there, but withers and dies away. All this will be very interesting for you to search into more particularly hereafter.

And equally interesting are the different ways in which pollination is brought about.

One of the most common ways, especially in monæcious and diæcious plants, is by the wind : the pollen being blown to and lodged upon the stigmas. If you have many yew trees in your neighbourhood, and can watch the clouds of pollen dust blown from the stamen bearing flowers, you will never again forget the agency of the wind in producing pollination. Other common instances are the hazel and Scotch fir. You may like to know that plants in which pollination is brought about mainly by the wind are called *anemophilous*,* or wind lovers.

But you must often have noticed bees and other insects busy in the flowers; that is another way in which pollination is very commonly brought about.

---

* From the Greek "*anemos*," wind; and "*phileo*," I love.

This is the cause, as some say the reason, of the bright colours, the fragrant perfume, and the sweet honey of so many of our flowers. These things attract the insects, and as they move about in the flower to collect the nectar,* or gather the pollen for food, the pollen sticks to their limbs and bodies, and is then brought into contact with the stigmas of the pistils as they move from flower to flower. You have a familiar instance of this in our common primroses, cowslips, and oxlips. In some the style is short, and the stigma about half way down the tube of the corolla, whilst the anthers are at the top of it (Fig. 110 A); but in others the style is long and the stigma at the top of the corolla tube, whilst the anthers are placed half way down it (Fig. 110, B). Suppose a bee enters one of the kinds of flowers, say the short styled one (Fig. A), to get the honey at the bottom of the corolla tube; as soon as it goes to one of the long styled flowers (Fig. B), that part of its body which touched the anthers before, and is dusted with their pollen, will now touch the stigma of the pistil and leave some of

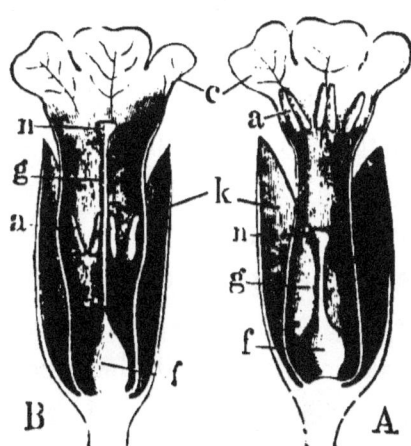

Fig. 110.—Flowers of Oxlip (*Primula elatior*), cf. Common Primrose (*P. vulgaris*).

---

* Nectar is immature honey.   cf. *nectary*, in the Appendix.

the pollen there. The pollen of the short styled flower A has been brought to the stigma of the long styled one B, and the like transfer is made as the bee goes on from B to A.

In Fig. 111 you can see a picture of a flower which shows another instance of insect pollination, and which has been interestingly described by Dr. Prantl and others. Notice how the lobes of the stigma (*n*) in the flower marked B are turned down over the anthers (*a*); and that the tube of the corolla has many hairs in it. As they all point downwards they do not hinder an insect from crawling down the tube; but when it has got the honey from the bottom of the tube and wants to come out again, the hairs then bar the way. But the visit of the insect, and its efforts to escape, are of great service to the flower in exchange for its honey. Pollen which it has brought on its body from some other flower of the same kind, will stick to the stigma, and the lobes of the stigma will turn upwards; and some of the pollen from the anthers below

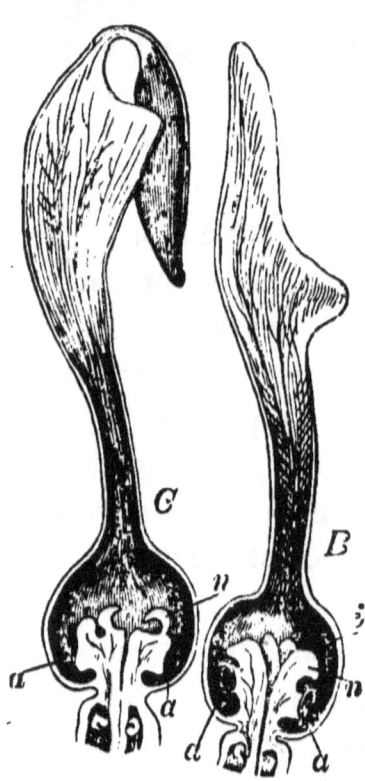

Fig. 111.—Flowers of Aristolochia. *B* before, *C* after pollination, *r* tube of perianth, *n* stigma, *a* anthers, *i* an insect, *lowest portion*, ovary with ovules.

will stick to the body of the insect as it crawls about in its efforts to escape. Then presently the hairs in the corolla tube wither away (Fig. 111C) and the insect escapes, carrying the pollen with it, which it will leave, in due course, upon the stigma of another flower. These plants to which the insects are so useful, and which generally have fragrant or bright coloured flowers, are called *entomophilous*,* or insect lovers.

But what takes place next to pollination? Then the pollen grain makes a very wonderful journey. If you look at Fig. 112 you can see a pollen grain very much magnified. You see that its outer coat is very much thinner at the points marked *a*, *b*, and *c*. Now at one of those points the pollen grain extends or grows out into a tube (Fig. 112 *s*), and so travels down the channel which I told you of (p. 128), through the stigma and style into the ovary until it reaches the ovule.† (Figs. 109 and 113.) But still its journey is not finished. It passes on through a channel in the ovule until it reaches a certain spot inside the ovule. (Fig. 109 and 113 at E.) This is called *fertilisation.*

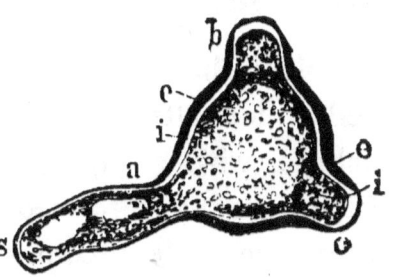

Fig. 112.—Pollen grain of Willow herb (*Epilobium*), much magnified. *e*, outer coat ; *i*, inner coat.

---

* From the Greek "*entoma*," insects, and "*phileo*," I love.

† In one division of flowering plants the ovules are not enclosed in ovaries ; the pollen falls at once upon the ovules.

Sometimes it happens very soon after pollination, but sometimes there is quite a long interval before it does so. But when fertilisation has taken place the ovules very greatly change. As a general rule the other parts of the flower, calyx, corolla, and stamens die away, and all the energy of the plant is given to the ovary or ovaries of the pistil, that the ovules within may be matured as seeds; for after fertilisation the young plant or embryo, with a supply of food for its first days of life, is gradually formed within the ovule. In other words, the ovule becomes changed into a seed, safely housed within the ovary; and the whole gradually ripens as *Fruit*. (Fig. 108.)

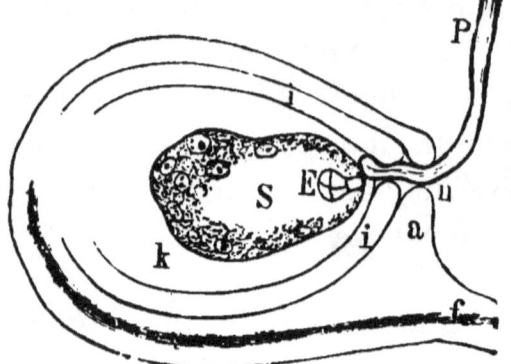

Fig. 113.—Ovule shortly after fertilisation. *P*, pollen tube; *i*, inner covering of the ovule, *k*; *S*, inner bag containing vital part of ovule at *E*, which has now become the embryo or germ of the seed; *f*, *funicle*, see Appendix.

CHAPTER XXIV.

FRUIT.

WE will begin by looking again at the fruit of the buttercup (Fig. 23, p. 27) or the primrose. Of course you can tell me what the fruit is? Quite right, it is the ripening pistil; the ovary and seeds of the primrose, or the ovaries and seed of the buttercup, as the case may be. It is a true fruit.

(1) But sometimes fruits are called *pseudo-carps*,* or *spurious* fruits. Such are the apple, or the strawberry, or the hips of a rose. For instance, if you take an apple and cut it in half, what do you see? After all the

Fig. 114.—Oak and acorns.

---

* From the Greek "*pseudos*," false (spurious), and "*karpos*," fruit.

apples you have eaten, I expect you know what it looks like very well. In the middle are the seeds, enclosed in the scaly carpels; then all round them is the tube of the calyx, or top of the flower stalk, which has swollen into the juicy part which in some apples is so good to eat. At the top of the apple you can see its dry and withered calyx (Fig. 25, p. 28). The apple then is not only the ripened pistil, but some other part of the flower is joined with it—the ripe pistil containing the seeds, that is, the true fruit, being enclosed in the swollen calyx tube or top of the flower stalk. That is why the apple is called a pseudocarp.

This joining of other parts of the flower to the ripe pistil happens in many different ways. Have you noticed in the strawberry the little brownish things which are upon it? People often think they are the seeds; but they are the true fruits, that is, the ripened ovaries containing the seed; and they are upon the swollen fleshy part which we like to eat; the whole making up a pseudocarp or spurious fruit (Fig. 115).

Fig. 115.—Strawberries.

In the hips of the wild rose, on the other hand, the true fruits are the hard, hairy little things which are *inside* the swollen calyx tube, or top of the flower stalk, instead of *outside* upon a fleshy pulp, as in the strawberry.

Other pseudocarps are the acorns with their cupules (Fig. 114), or the beech nuts with their husks; and there are many others.

But you can now tell the difference between true fruits and pseudocarps. The true fruit is simply the ripened pistil, *i.e.*, the ovary, or ovaries, with the seed; but when some other part of the flower is combined with the pistil, the fruit is distinguished as a pseudocarp.

But there are some other general differences between fruits which you must notice; and then I shall be able to tell you the names by which the particular kinds of fruit are called.

(2) So we will notice next the difference between *simple, compound,* and *collective* fruits.

The difference between a simple and a compound fruit is one which you already know. For, since fruits are the ripened pistils of flowers, they are divided, as pistils are, into simple, apocarpous, or syncarpous. *Simple,* as the pea or bean (Fig. 15 *d*, p. 21); *apocarpous,* as the buttercup (Fig. 23, p. 27), the monkshood (Fig. 161), the columbine, the raspberry (Fig. 22, p. 26), and the blackberry; *syncarpous,* as in the poppy (Figs. 26, p. 30; 123*c*), the cowslip, and the primrose. Try and find these and other examples of these different kinds of fruits, or ripened pistils: and if you do not quite understand them read again about the pistil in Ch. XXI. I need only add that an apocarpous or syncarpous fruit, since it is formed from a pistil of more than one carpel is often called *compound* to distinguish it from a simple fruit, which is formed from a pistil of one carpel only.

Each of these fruits that we have been speaking about is formed, as you know, from a single flower. But sometimes a fruit is formed from several flowers. The common fig is a well-known example of this kind of fruit, and as easy as any for you to understand. The flowers of the fig tree are very curiously placed. The flower stalk is hollowed out into a kind of fleshy bag or receptacle, and the flowers are arranged inside it. Cut open a fig whilst it is young and green, and see if you can distinguish them. In due course the flowers produce their fruits, and these are the little grains so familiar to us in the pulp of the ripened fig. So the skin of the fig is part of the expanded flower stalk; (the fig is therefore a pseudocarp)— and inside are the collected fruits of all its many flowers. So this kind of fruit is called a *collective* fruit, to distinguish it from those fruits which are formed only from a single flower (Fig. 116). Other examples of collective fruits are the fir cone (Fig. 117), the hop, the mulberry, and the

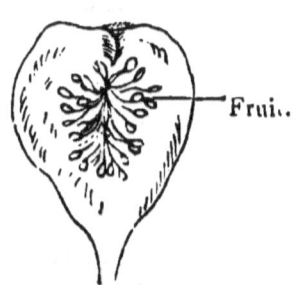

Fig. 116.—Collective fruit of Fig. Pseudocarp. Fruits enclosed in hollowed peduncle.

pineapple. You will study them when you are older. Now if we can find a blackberry or wild raspberry (Figs. 133, 22, p. 26), what kind of fruit is it? Yes! not a collective but an apocarpous fruit: for it is all formed from a single flower, and each little fruit or ripened ovary of which it is made up is called a *fruitlet.* *

Fig. 117.—Fir branch with cones.

Fig 118.—Collective fruit of Mulberry.

(3) For the next distinction between fruits, we must notice the case or covering in which the seed is enclosed. It is called the *pericarp.*† Sometimes the pericarp is so thickened that it can be divided into three distinct layers: the outside one, or *epicarp* ;† the middle one, or *mesocarp* ;† and the inner one, or *endocarp*† (Fig. 119). The pericarp

---

* When you have an opportunity compare the fruit of the mulberry with that of the blackberry. For in the mulberry each part or division is the spurious fruit of a distinct flower: and so the whole is a collective fruit (Figs. 118, 133).

† From the Greek "*peri,*" around ; "*epi,*" upon ; "*mesos,*" middle ; "*endon,*" within ; and "*karpos,*" fruit. See "*sarcocarp,*" in the Appendix.

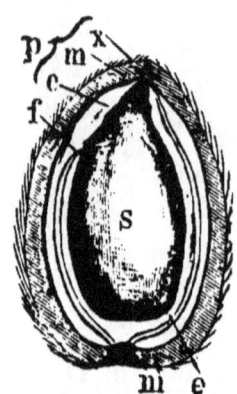

Fig. 119.—Fruit of an Almond tree. Longitudinal section (cut in half lengthways). *s* the seed, *e* endocarp, *m* mesocarp, *x* epicarp, all making up *p* the pericarp, *f* the funicle.

varies a good deal in character: sometimes it is dry, but part of it is often soft and juicy; so fruits are dry or succulent according to the nature of their pericarp.

Now I will tell you some examples, and we will find as many of them as we can. The pericarp is dry, and hard or leathery, in the hazel nut, buttercup, vetch, bean, radish, and poppy; and these are *dry* fruits.

But think of the plum, apricot, peach, or cherry. In these you have the thin epicarp or outside skin, then the soft juicy part you like to eat, which is the mesocarp; whilst the shell of the stone is the hardened endocarp (Fig. 120) These, therefore, are *succulent* fruits; so also are the grape, the currant, and the date, in which both mesocarp and endocarp are soft and pulpy, the seed or seeds being imbedded in them.

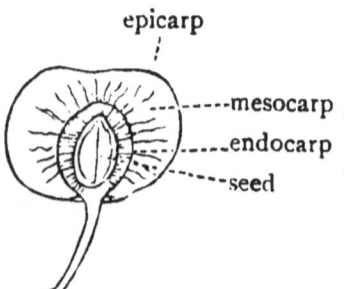

Fig. 120.—Fruit of Cherry (cut in half).

Be careful not to confuse the skin of the fig, or the hip of the rose, with the pericarp of the fruit, for these as you know, are pseudocarps, and have the fruits with their hard dry pericarps inside them.

(4) And now, last of all, I want you to notice how the seeds become free from the ovary case, or pericarp. For when the pericarp opens so as to let the seed escape, the fruits are called *dehiscent*.* If the seed case splits open lengthways the parts into which it splits are called "*valves*," and the dehiscence is *longitudinal;* compare this in the iris, monk's hood (Fig. 161), pea, or wallflower (*cf.* Fig. 121). And notice the little teeth with which the seed case sometimes opens at the upper end, as in the primrose, cowslip, or the chickweed.

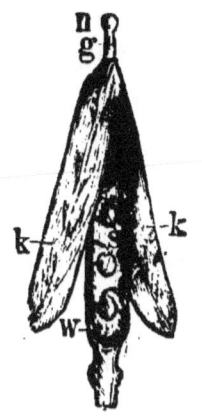

Fig. 121.—Fruit of Brassica (*siliqua*). *k* the valves, *w* dissepiment, *s* seeds, *g* style, *n* stigma.

If we can find a little pimpernel (poor man's weather glass) with its seed ripe, we shall see that its seed case opens in another way; it splits across and the top comes off. This is called *transverse* dehiscence. (*cf.* Fig. 130.) But sometimes the seed case opens with little holes as in the poppy: these openings are called *pores*, and the dehiscence is *porous*. (Fig. 122.)

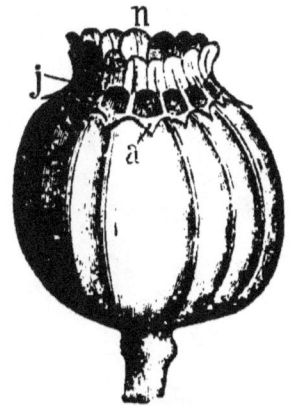

Fig. 122.—Fruit (*capsule*) of Poppy (*Papaver somniferum*), opening by pores. *n*, stigma; *j*, the pores which open by the removal of the valves, *a*.

Sometimes, however, the pericarp does not open to let

---

* From the Latin "*dehisco*," "*dehiscens*," gaping, opening.

the seed escape; but either gradually rots away from the seed, or the seed bursts through it when it begins to grow: the fruit is then called *indehiscent.**
Such are the fruits of the currant, gooseberry, cherry, or hazel.

When the fruits are ripening and the days are fine, take pains to find examples of these differences and try and understand them well, working also through the list in the next chapter of some common names by which different kinds of fruit are known.

---

* From the Latin "*indehisco*," "*indehiscens*," not gaping or opening.

CHAPTER XXV.

DIFFERENT KINDS OF FRUIT.

Fig. 123.—Poppy (*Papaver*), with syncarpous chambered capsule at *c*.

IN the later summer days, when the fruits are ripening, you will now be able to work through the following list of the most common kinds of simple and compound fruit.

I.—*Dry* fruits (generally *dehiscent* and *many seeded*).

(1) The *legume* * or *pod* is a simple fruit (p. 137), which opens along both sutures, dorsal and ventral, so that it splits into halves. Sometimes the legume is twisted. Sometimes it is jointed or narrowed between the seeds, as in the bird's foot (*Ornithopus*). It is then called a *lomentum* † (Fig. 173). It does

---

* From the Latin "*legumen*" (fr. "*lego*," I gather), pulse, peas, beans &c., gathered by hand.

† From the Latin "*lomentum*," bean meal.

144 FLOWER-LAND.

not burst open like the legume, though it breaks or separates at the joints. Common examples of the legume are the pea, furze, bean, and other papilionaceæ F ig. 15, p. 21).

(2) The *follicle** is a fruitlet of an apocarpous (compound) fruit, and formed of a single carpel, which dehisces along the ventral suture (Fig. 124), as in the columbine, larkspur, and monks' hood (Fig. 161 *e*).

Fig. 124.—A Follicle.

(3) *Siliqua and silicula.*
The *siliqua*† is a syncarpous (compound) fruit, of two carpels and with a partition (dissepiment) between them. It dehisces from the base upwards, the two carpels splitting away from the partition, which remains erect on the top of the peduncle. Examples are the wall-flower, mustard and other cruciferæ (Fig. 125).

Fig. 125—Siliqua of Brassica. *v* dissepiment (*cf.* Fig. 121).

Fig. 126.—Silicle of Whitlow grass (*Draba*) dehiscing. E, transverse section; *v*, dissepiment; *s*, seed.

When the shape of it is short and broad, it is a *silicula*,‡

---

* From the Latin "*folliculus*," a little bag.
† From the Latin "*siliqua*," a husk.
‡ From the Latin "*silicula*," a little husk.

or *silicle*, as in the shepherd's purse (*Capsella*), cress, and others of the cruciferæ (*cf.* Figs. 126, 127). The fruits are sometimes *lomentaceous* (p. 143), as in the radish (Fig. 128).

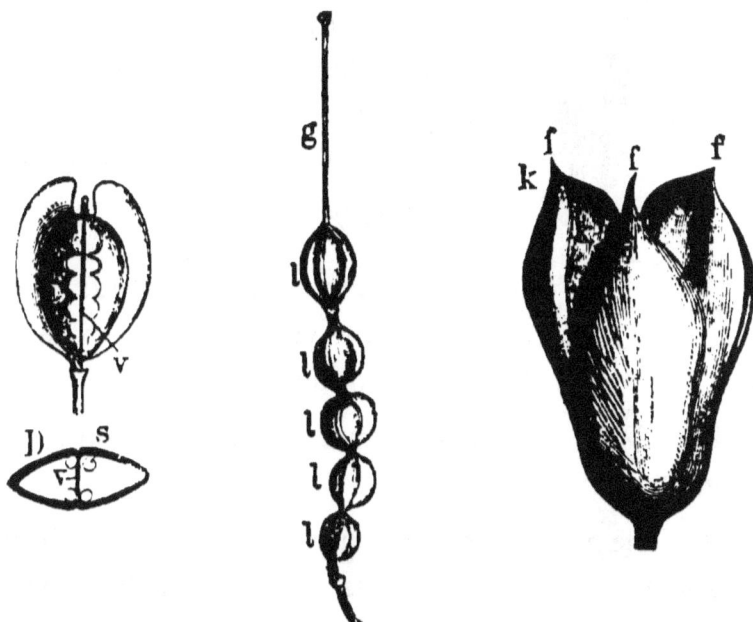

Fig. 127.—Silicle of Penny cress (*Thlaspi*). D, transverse section; *v*, dissepiment; *s*, seed.

Fig. 128.—Lomentaceous siliqua of Radish (*Raphanus*). *l*, the separate segments; *g*, the style.

Fig. 129.—Capsule of Autumn crocus (*Colchicum autumnale*). *f*, the three separating carpels; *k*, the valves.

(4) The *capsule** is a syncarpous fruit, which may be unilocular or multilocular (p. 119), when it dehisces lengthways (longitudinal dehiscence), it sometimes splits all the way down or nearly so (*cf.* Figs. 129, 140), or only at the top, forming notches or teeth, as in the primrose, cowslip, chickweed (*Cerastium*) or campion (*Lychnis*). *cf. Dehiscence* in the Appendix.

---

* From the Latin "*capsula*," a little chest.

When the capsule opens across the top like the lid of a box, it is called a *pyxidium* * (transverse dehiscence p. 141). Look for the pretty little pimpernel (*Anagallis*) for a good example of the pyxidium, or you find it in the fruit of the henbane (*Hyoscyamus*) (Fig. 130). Compare also the capsule of the common plantain (*Plantago*).

Fig. 130.—Pyxidium of Henbane (*Hyoscyamus*). *d*, the lid; *w*, dissepiment; *s*, seeds.

The *pore capsule* (Fig. 122, p. 141) you know very well, I expect, in the poppy or the snapdragon (*Antirrhinum*).

II.—*Dry* and *Indehiscent* fruits (generally *one-seeded*).

(1) The *achene*† is a superior one-seeded simple fruit or fruitlet of an apocarpous (compound) fruit, with a thin pericarp; the fruit of the buttercup is a good example.

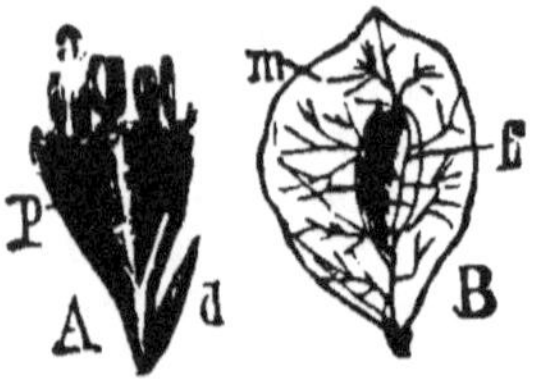

The fruitlets inside the pseudocarp of the wild rose and those on the outside of the pseudocarp of the strawberry are also achenes. (*Cf. caryopsis, cypsela, samara* (Fig. 131, in Appendix C.)

Fig. 131.—*A*, Flower of Elm (*Ulmus campestris*); *d*, bract; *p*, perianth; *a*, stamens. *B*, fruit (*samara*); *f*, achene with *m* membranous margin.

(2) The *nut* is truly a syncarpous (compound) fruit, generally one-seeded, and, when ripe, it has a hard,

---

* From the Latin "*pyxis*," a box.

† From the Greek "*a*," not, and "*kaino*," I open.

scaly, or bony pericarp. Compare hazel nut, beech nut,* and acorn (Figs. 103h, p. 121; 114, p. 135). The nut often changes greatly as it is formed from the ovary into fruit. The hazel, for instance, has a bilocular ovary, but one cell is barren, and so the fruit is unilocular (one-celled); and it is generally one-seeded.†

Before passing on to succulent fruits we must notice the *schizocarp*. Sometimes as a syncarpous (compound) fruit ripens, the loculi develop so that each one is a complete seed-box, and then they divide into separate fruitlets. This kind of separating syncarpous fruit is called a *schizocarp*.‡

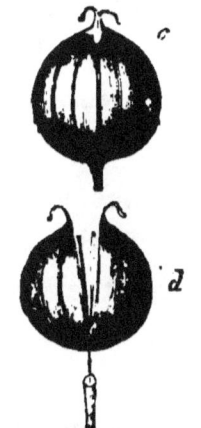

Fig 132.—Mericarp of Caraway (*Carum*).

If the separated fruitlets are only two in number, each is called a *mericarp*‡: as in the cow-parsnip (*Heracleum sphondylium*) and the other umbelliferæ (Fig. 132). Sometimes there are more than two fruitlets, as in the common Herb-Robert (*Geranium Robertianum*) (*cf.* Fig. 141).

---

* In the pseudocarp of the beech (*Fagus*), the cupule or husk containing the nuts is a bract-like involucre to the flowers, which has remained as a cupule to their fruits, *i.e.*, the nuts, each nut being the fruit of a separate flower.

† You should cut across the ovaries of the hazel, beech, or oak, and try with your magnifying glass to see the loculi or cells. The oak has a trilocular (three celled) ovary, with two ovules in each cell; but all the cells and ovules come to nothing except one cell with one ovule, which becomes the acorn.

‡ From the Greek "*schizo*," I divide, or "*meros*," a part or share; and "*karpos*," fruit (*cf. coccus*, in Appendix C).

III.—*Succulent* fruits (generally *indehiscent*).

(1) The *drupe** is a simple or syncarpous (compound) fruit, with a fleshy mesocarp, and hard or stony endocarp. You know it well, and perhaps it is one of your favourite fruits, as it includes the plum, the cherry (Fig. 120), the peach, the apricot, and other kinds of stone fruit, as they are often called.

Fig. 133.—Drupaceous Fruit of Blackberry. *d*, drupels.

Here you must notice some drupaceous apocarpous (compound) fruits, such as the blackberry and the raspberry: each ripened ovary or fruitlet being called a *drupel* or *little drupe* (Figs. 133, 22, p. 26).

So also the drupaceous, but syncarpous walnut. Get the whole fruit, if possible, fresh off the tree, and take the hard endocarp, with the seed inside it, out of its green case, that is, the fleshy mesocarp, with its thin skin or epicarp. Only be careful, if you do not want to stain your fingers; and if you taste the mesocarp, you will not, I think, be inclined to taste it again; unless, indeed, you enjoy the whole fruit—epicarp, mesocarp, endocarp, and seed, pickled when young or tender—pickled walnuts.†

---

* From the Latin "*drupæ*" (from the Greek "*drys*," a tree, and "*pipto*," I fall), ripe olives, ready to fall off.

† Compare the drupaceous walnuts with the nuts of the hazel or beech (p. 147).

(2) The *berry* has a thin epicarp or skin, but all the rest of the pericarp is succulent, surrounding the seed—as the gooseberry, the currant, the grape, and the cucumber. Berries are one or many seeded, and one or many celled, and some have special names, amongst which are the cucumbers and gourds.*

Perhaps you prefer the date (Fig. 134) to the cucumber or vegetable marrow. That, too, is a berry —a one-seeded berry—for that which is commonly called a date stone is not a stone with a kernel (*i.e.*, a hard endocarp enclosing the seed), like that of the plum (a drupe), but it is the kernel or seed itself enclosed by its soft pericarp, and a very hard and stony seed it is.

There are two other common but favourite fruits which are allied to the berry—the orange and the lemon. In these fruits the pericarp is the well-known "peel" with its pith-like inner layer. As the fruit ripens the cells of the ovary become filled with the sweet succulent pulp which we like to eat. You have often peeled an orange, I expect, and separated and eaten its juicy carpel bags.

It is worth while to cut an orange in half transversely, *i.e.*, cut the top part off, so as to see these cells of the ovary containing the seeds.

If you have an opportunity, and can get it without tumbling into the water, the fruit of the yellow water lily is well worth notice. Dr. Goebel has called it

---

* *Cf.* Appendix C., Berry.

a *dehiscent berry;* the carpels separate and each loculus becomes like a little berry.

But I have told you enough to occupy you amongst fruits for some little time. Their varieties are very many, and do not be disheartened if you find some which puzzle you. Learn well now the simpler kinds about which I have told you, and you will understand the more puzzling fruits better as you become more experienced.*

---

* In due time you can learn some special names which have been given to some spurious and collective fruits. (*cf.* Appendix C.)

CHAPTER XXVI.

SEEDS.

Fig. 134.—The Date Palm.

IT will be on some of the dry days of autumn that you will best be able to explore amongst the seeds of our common English plants. But very many of them are small; so small that you cannot really see them well without a microscope, and I want you to know something more about seeds before the autumn comes. So let us try and get a grain or two of wheat, a few peas or beans, one or two prunes, dates, and walnuts, an apple, a Brazil nut, a common hazel nut or filbert, a pear, an orange, and a nutmeg; and we will grind the nutmeg partly away upon a grater. Then we will talk about them in the evening, or when it is a wet day, and you cannot go out.

Now as we place our little store before us, we will cut open the apple (Fig. 25, p. 28), and the orange, and the pear, and get out their seeds or pips as we call them. And what about the seeds of the walnut, prune, and date? Yes! the hard stony thing inside the date fruit is its seed: but in the prune or dried plum you have to crack the stone (the endocarp) and then you can get out the seed, that is the kernel. So also with the shell or pericarp of the nut and the endocarp of the walnut (p. 148). And we will get a little water and put a pea and bean in it that they may soak a little.

Now let us take this walnut seed or kernel, and peel off the thin skin which covers it. This skin, or coat of the seed is called *the testa* * (Fig. 135 *s*), and varies much in different seeds. You can see by looking at the seeds before us how different it is in colour. In the apple it is a rich dark brown, a lighter shade of brown in the prune, in the orange seed it is white, in the pear black, in the common mustard it is yellow. When you have an opportunity of looking at some of our common wild flower seeds under the microscope, you will find some of

---

* From the Latin "*testa*," a jar, a cask (the shell or covering of the seed).

them with very pretty patterns; and sometimes the pattern is in colours, as in the seed of the common campion (*Lychnis*).

So also you will find a wonderful variety as to the smoothness or roughness of the seed coats. Sometimes, like those of the bean or apple, they are smooth to touch; but in many seeds they are rough with knobs, or furrowed, or winged, or tufted, or rough with hairs.

And as to substance, see how thin and membranous is this testa or skin of the walnut seed. Try that of the bean. It has softened I dare say in the water, and as you peel off its coat you find that it is thicker and more leathery than that of the walnut.

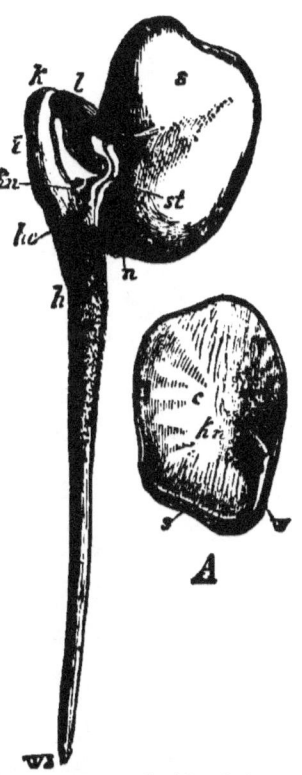

Fig. 135.—*A*, half of bean seed. *kn* plumule of embryo, *w* its radicle, *c* one of the cotyledons, *s* the testa.

These differences evidently depend upon the character of the pericarp in which the seeds are enclosed. When the seed remains safely in the pericarp until it begins to grow, then the testa is likely to be thin and tender; but if the pericarp is soft so that the seed might be easily damaged, or if it dehisces and the seeds are sent out to fare as best they may, then the testa becomes hard, or tough, or hairy, &c., that it may protect the little plant inside it.

So now split some of these seeds in half. Perhaps you cannot see anything very distinctly, only a whitish mass; but you know that this substance of the seed is a store of food for the embryo, or little plant, which is embedded in it (p. 134). If you do not quite remember about the embryo, we will turn back and read again about its radicle and plumule (p. 65, 71), and its seed leaves, either one or two (p. 33). These seed leaves are called *cotyledons*.* Sometimes they are large and fleshy, take up all the store of food into themselves, and fill up the testa, as in the bean (Fig. 135,) or almond (Fig. 136, C.) But in Fig.

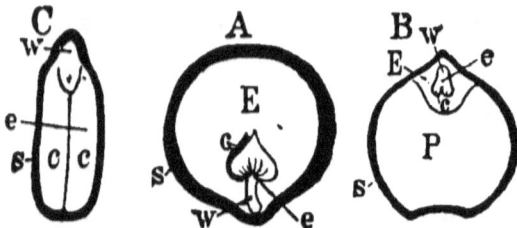

Fig. 136.—Sections of ripe seeds. *A*, nux vomica; *B*, piper; *C*, almond; *s*, testa; *e*, embryo; *w*, its radicle; *c*, cotyledons. For *E* and *P*, see note.†

136, *A* and *B*, you see pictures of seeds cut in half, in which the cotyledons remain small, and the whole embryo is surrounded by its food, which fills up the rest of the testa.†

---

* From the Greek, "*kotylēdōn*," a hollow like a cup; from "*kotylē*," a cup.

† *Cf.* Appendix. *Endosperm, perisperm.*

We have now to notice how the substance or body of the seed varies both in hardness and in shape. So compare the peculiarly crumpled or folded seed of the walnut with the other variously shaped but smooth and even seeds which are before you. And look at your nutmeg. Do you see how its substance is mottled? That is caused by a layer of the testa, which grows in and out between the folded substance or body of the seed. And its substance is very hard also. In the pip of the apple or kernel of the nut, on the other hand, it is softer. In the date seed, however, whilst its testa is very fragile, its body or substance is harder than in the nutmeg: so hard that you may use knife or hammer upon it, and not easily make much impression. Yet the little date plant which it surrounds feeds and thrives upon it when the date seeds are planted and begin to grow.

Will you crack the Brazil nut? How oily this seed is. You can not only *taste* this, but, if you squeeze a bit of it hard, you will *see* that it is so. And if you can get one whole out of its shell, and cut it to a point at one end, and light it, it will burn freely. It is a complete little lamp—wick and oil and lamp together.

Whilst it is burning, eat the wheat seed slowly. Does it not remind you of flour and bread?

Very different again is the nutmeg. Scrape or grate it a little, and notice how fragrant it is; and you know that some people are fond of it as a spice or flavouring.

So you have oil and flour and spice, all close at hand. I think you will find the different ways in which seeds are useful to us a very interesting part of botany.

But how wonderful is the production of seed. Wonderful if we think of a flower that produces but a single seed, as the common nut. Wonderful if we think of such a flower as the poppy, a fruit of which has been found to contain up to 40,000 seeds; 40,000 cases containing little poppy germs, each capable of growing into root, and stem, and leaves, and flower, and fruit, and 40,000 seeds again!

CHAPTER XXVII.

DISTRIBUTION OF SEEDS.

Fig. 137.—Fool's Parsley (*Æthusa cynapium*), with reflexed bracts.

I WONDER if you can tell me what all the life of a plant is working for? Why plants and their parts are found in all these different forms and colours which you have been learning about? Yes, the root, the stem, the leaves, and all their wonderful variety, work together that plants may live. They are the "organs of nourishment." Then the energy of the living plants spends itself in forming flowers and fruits—with all their wonderful variety—the "organs of reproduction." So that the great business of plants is to produce their seed by which their kind may be kept alive upon the earth after those of any particular generation are dead and gone. I should like you to remember this. So notice again how wonderfully the seeds are covered and protected by pericarp or testa, or by both (p. 152). And then on fine summer days let us search to find out some of the wonderful ways in which plants take pains that their seeds may ripen safely, and, when ripe, may be "scattered," or "sown."

Notice, for instance, the common dandelion in full bloom, how conspicuous it is, its stalk erect, and its bright yellow florets all wide open.

But presently the involucre will close up around its withering florets, and the flower stalk (scape, p. 107) will bend downwards with the precious head of fertilised ovules, so that they may become seeds (p. 134) ripe and ready to be sown. Then up rises its stalk again, and its involucre opens wide, and the head of fruits, each with a feathery tail attached to it,* is raised high, so that the fruits with their precious seed may be scattered by the wind. Have you never seen children blowing at these feathery heads or "clocks" as they are called, to see

---

* This is called a "*pappus*," see Fig. 138, *a, b, e*.

in how many puffs they can blow off all the feathery fruits? (Fig. 138 *a*.) Try one now. First notice the little fruits or inferior achenes (cypselas) with their feathery tails (Fig. 138 *b*, *e*), and then start them on their journey through the air, and watch how admirably

Fig. 138.—Dandelion (*Leontodon*); *a*, head of seeds; *b*, head with all seeds removed but one, showing reflexed involucre, pitted receptacle and one fruit with pappus; *e*, one fruit with pappus magnified; *c*, receptacle with one floret left upon it; *d*, floret magnified, showing ovary at base, the hairy calyx which becomes the pappus, the tubular corolla with expanded limb (ligulate), the anthers of the stamens being close around the style of the pistil, of which the stigma at the top is notched.

the plant has produced that which will bring about what is desired, that its ripe seeds should be scattered that the dandelion plants may spread and grow from year to year.

You will find many other fruits and seeds which have appendages that they may be wafted by the wind. Either feathery hairs as in the willow-herb, cotton grass, thistles and other composite plants, clematis and bulrush; or a thin membrane, or wing, as in the maple or sycamore (*cf.* Figs. 28 *b*, p. 33; 139).

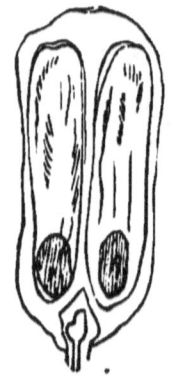

Fig. 139.—Scale of fruit of Scotch Fir, showing two winged seeds.

Sometimes the seeds are scattered by what Sir John Lubbock describes as "innocent artillery." That is, plants throw out their seeds, sometimes to a considerable distance, by the contraction or expansion of the seed case (*cf.* Fig. 140). There is a plant which grows in moist places in the north of England, called the yellow balsam. If you touch its fruit when it is ripe, the valves of the seed vessel will spring off and scatter the seeds to a considerable distance; so the plant is called "*Impatiens-noli-me-tangere*," *i.e.*, "I am impatient (of being touched), do not touch me."

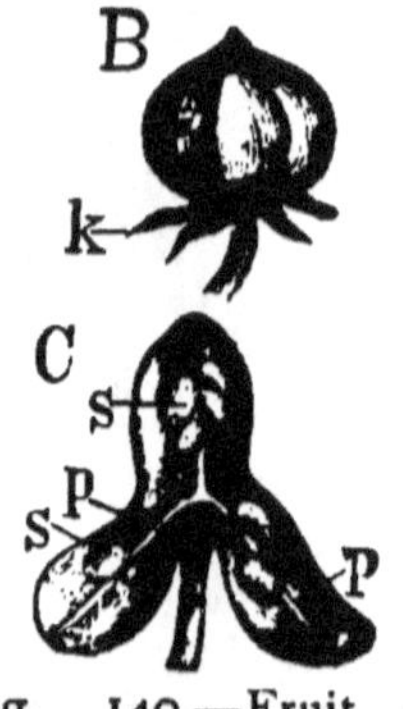

Fig. 140.—Fruit of Pansy Violet (*Viola tricolor*); *B*, ripe fruit; *k*, calyx; *C*, fruit after dehiscence; *p*, placentæ; *s*, seeds.

In the common Herb-Robert, each of the five fruitlets has a long thin projection which reaches from the

DISTRIBUTION OF SEEDS.

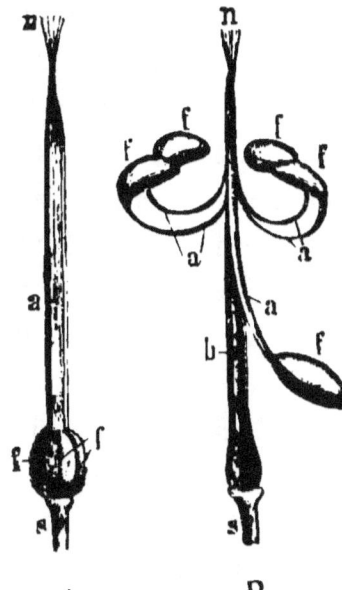

Fig. 141.—Fruit of Geranium. *A*, before dehiscence; *B*, after dehiscence; *s*, pedicel; *f*, loculi of the ovary which is prolonged into a beak *a*; *b* shows the central column remaining after dehiscence; *n*, the stigma.

ovary or seed case to the top (*apex*) of the central axis or flower stalk. These rods become tightly stretched when the seeds are ripe, so tightly that at length they burst away, and as they do so jerk to a considerable distance the five little fruits or carpels containing the seed (Fig. 141). On warm autumn days you may hear the pods of many of the butterfly plants bursting and scattering the seeds, as also the siliquas (p. 144) of the Cruciferæ (cross bearers). In the stork's bill, another species of the geranium order, the seeds are scattered as in the Herb-Robert.

Some seeds have a twisted rod or awn something like a corkscrew. If the weather is damp, the rod untwists and lengthens; if dry, it contracts again; and so, as some think, the seed is enabled to travel some little distance. Others, however, think that this movement is for the purpose of forcing the seed into the ground.

If you walk through a wood you will probably carry out the wishes of certain kinds of plants in distributing their seeds. Have you never found the little round balls of the harriff (hair rough) clinging to your clothes? They are its fruits, furnished with little hooks (p. 23), so that they stick to you, or to the rabbit or the dog that brushes past them, and are carried off to found elsewhere a new colony of harriff. Hence the common name which has been given them of "cleavers." Perhaps you have been troubled with the larger fruits and stronger hooks of the seed vessels of the hound's tongue (*Cynoglossum*), a plant with downy leaves and dull red flowers. If you look at these fruits through the microscope (with a low magnifying power), you will see many of the hooks with five spreading teeth curved downwards and inwards. Very formidable they look, and one no longer wonders that they are so difficult to get rid of from one's clothes.

In some foreign plants the hooks of the fruits are so large and strong that they are said even to kill lions. As these hooked fruits roll about over the dry plains, they sometimes become attached to the lion's skin. "The wretched animal tries to tear them out, and, sometimes getting them into his mouth, perishes miserably."*

You can find other instances of those hooked fruits in the enchanter's nightshade *(circæa)*, and the hedge parsley *(torilis)*.

Such are some, and only some, of the ways in

---

* Sir John Lubbock, in "Flowers, Fruits, and Leaves."

which seeds are dispersed and sown. How marvellous and full of interest it is to search and find out the wonders of plants: the wonderful ways in which they not only produce, but also provide for the distribution of, their seeds.

ANATOMY.

CHAPTER XXVIII.

CELLS, VESSELS, AND TISSUES.

Fig. 142.—Head of Teasel (*Dipsacus sylvestris*), with involucral bracts.

WE are now going to search just a very little into a branch of Botany which is more difficult than what you have been learning hitherto. So far we have been talking chiefly about the parts of Flowering Plants as they appear to us in their outward forms—the Morphology of plants.

But now break or cut a buttercup stem across, or the stem of a stinging nettle, if you can do so without being stung, or a branch of a shrub or tree. Look at a bit of board which you know has been sawn out of the trunk of some tree; break the stalk of a dandelion; cut an apple or plum in half, or tear across one or two different kinds of leaves. How different the substance of these things! Now I want to-day to tell you a little about how these things, and all other parts of plants, are made up.

You cannot make out very much as you look at the soft, sappy substance of the buttercup stem, or the hard wood, or the thin or fleshy leaves. To search into them thoroughly requires a microscope; but with the use of your magnifying glass and a few pictures, we shall be very well able to understand something about the composition of plants and their parts: the way in which they are made up—the Anatomy * of Plants.

We shall begin with an orange. Choose the ripest you can find: partly cut, and then tear it in half. Now, the pulp is made up of a lot of little juicy bags or bladders. Separate a little bit of it carefully, and you will easily get one or two of these little bladders unbroken. They are called "cells," and cells are the first or foundation substance of which plants are made up. But these cells of the orange pulp are old ones. Their life is over; they are simply bags full of juice—a pulpy covering for the seeds—and in due course they would rot away. But in its young and

---

* From the Greek "*ana*" and "*temno*," I cut in pieces, I separate.

growing state the cell contains a soft substance, alive; that is, with power of growth, which is called "*protoplasm.*" * In these plants which you are learning about, it has a special part called a *nucleus;* its skin or covering is the *cell wall,* and the watery fluid which is found in cells is called the *cell sap,* about which I will tell you a little more in due course.

Now, how do cells increase in number? When you learn about the flowerless plants, you will find that sometimes old cells become young again, or two

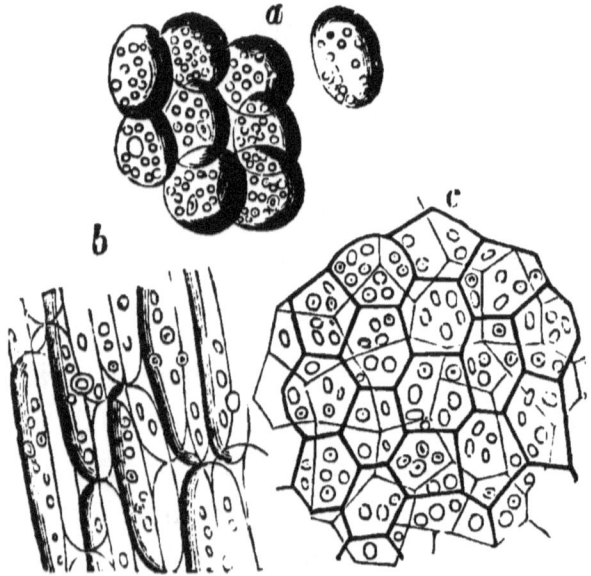

Fig. 143.—Various kinds of cellular tissue (*parenchyma*).

or more join together to form a new cell: but now remember that cells increase in number by division. You will learn in due course about the different ways

---

* From the Greek "*protos,*" first, and "*plasma,*" anything moulded or modelled.

in which they may divide; but generally the nucleus and protoplasm divide into parts, and a new cell wall is formed between them, so that there are two cells instead of one.* Thus the division goes on, and a collection of cells is formed, which is called *tissue;* and so the whole plant is developed, or grows up, from "cells."

The simplest form of tissue is made up of simple cells. It is therefore called *cellular tissue*, and is of two kinds according to the general shape of the cells of which it is composed. If we were to get some of the pith of the elder,† we should find that it was made up of a lot of cells about as long as they are broad. These are called "short cells," and such a tissue is called "*parenchyma*"‡ (Fig. 143).

But if we carefully separated the parts of a stem, we should find in it long and narrow cells. These overlap one another and so form a stiff tissue, which, though long and narrow, is able to stand upright and carry weight, as in the stem of a buttercup. This kind of tissue,

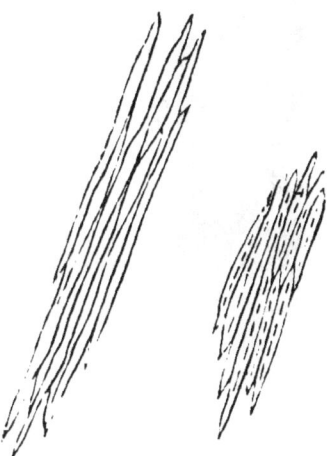

Fig. 144.—Cellular tissue (*prosenchyma*).

---

* *cf.* Cell in the Appendix.
† Try this with your magnifying glass; also pith of dahlia.
‡ From the Greek "*para*," beside, and "*encheo*," to pour in.

made up of the long cells, is called "*prosenchyma*"*
(Fig. 144).

In some parts of stems, however, you find another kind of tissue. In a pile or column of cells, one on the top of the other, the divisions between them sometimes gradually disappear, or partly so, so that there is a free passage from end to end of the whole column or set of cells, and so is formed a long tube or "*vessel.*" The sides or walls of these vessels differ a good deal according to the way in which the original cell divisions or walls have been removed or altered. I will only tell you that the

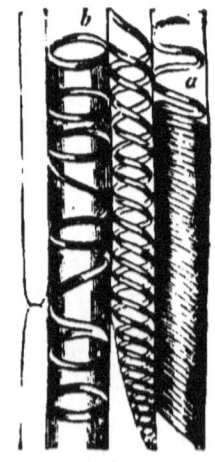

Fig. 145.—Spiral vessels.

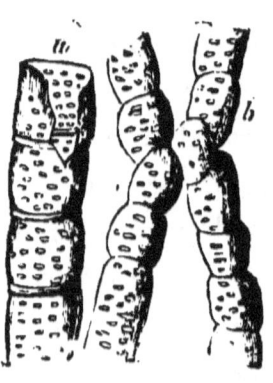

Fig. 146.—Pitted vessels.

most common ones are known as *ringed (annular)*†, or *spiral*, or *pitted*, or *scalariform* ‡ according to these differences in their walls (Figs. 145, 146, 147). You

---

* From the Greek "*pros,*" to, and "*encheo,*" to pour in.

† From the Latin "*annulus,*" a ring, a curled lock of hair.

‡ From the Latin "*scalaris*" (*scala*) of a ladder, and "*forma,*" shape or form.

CELLS, VESSELS, AND TISSUES.

may perhaps find some of them for yourself out of a piece of rhubarb, when next you have any rhubarb

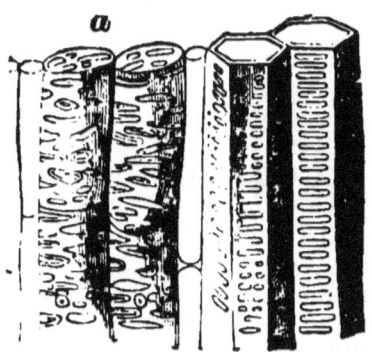

Fig. 147.—Scalariform vessels (on the right hand).

tart for dinner. You must tear a very small piece into shreds with a pin or needle, and then try what you can see with your magnifying glass. Under the microscope you would see it as in the picture (Fig. 148). Now a tissue made up of vessels is called *vascular tissue.** So now you know that it is of cellular tissue (parenchyma or prosenchyma) and of vascular tissue that these flowering plants and their parts are made up.

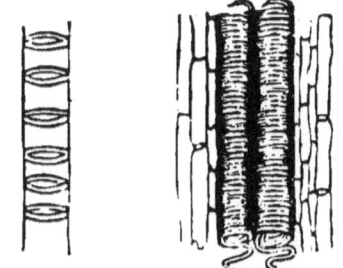

Fig. 148.—Annular vessel, and spiral vessels from rhubarb.

Notice how the shape of cells and the spaces between them † vary according to the closeness with

---

* From the Latin "*vasculum*" (*vas*), a vessel.

† These are called "intercellular spaces," from the Latin "*inter*," between (the cells).

which they are joined together in the tissue (Figs. 143, 149).

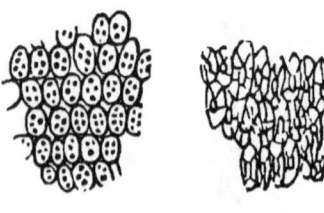

Fig. 149.—*Left hand* shows bark cells from horse chestnut, *right hand* hard cells from stone of damson (*sclerenchyma*).

And notice also how cells change as they grow old and die. There are not only the soft and juicy cells of the yellow orange pulp, or the soft and dry ones of the pith of trees, but sometimes they harden as they dry up so as to form hard tissue* like that of bark, or wood, or the stone of a plum or peach (Fig. 149).

---

* *cf. sclerenchyma*, Appendix.

CHAPTER XXIX.

TISSUES.

Fig. 150.—Spike of Grass.
a, a single flower.

As we are going to talk about *tissues*, I shall begin by asking you to tell me what a tissue is (p. 167).

(1) So now we will take a tissue of the simplest form— some cells joined only end to end. You will find examples in many hairs. If you look again at Fig. 54, p. 81, you will see some hairs magnified, which are made up of cells joined only end to end.

(2) Now suppose you have a lot of cells placed together, like a single layer of eggs upon a table, and which have grown together, so that they form a thin sheet or skin of cells. There is just such a skin or tissue of cells covering the surface of the parts of plants, and enclosing the other tissues within it.* It is, therefore, called the *epidermal† tissue*, or simply the *epidermis†*; and it generally consists of a single layer of cells, as I have described it. The outside walls of the epidermal cells are more or less thickened and hardened, and grow together so as to form the surface skin or outside wall, which is called the *cuticle*.‡ You can see a picture of the epidermis and its cuticle in Fig. 151. Try if you can distinguish it in a thickish leaf, or some herbaceous stem; or try for it upon an onion bulb. In the stems and shoots of shrubs and trees, the green and tender

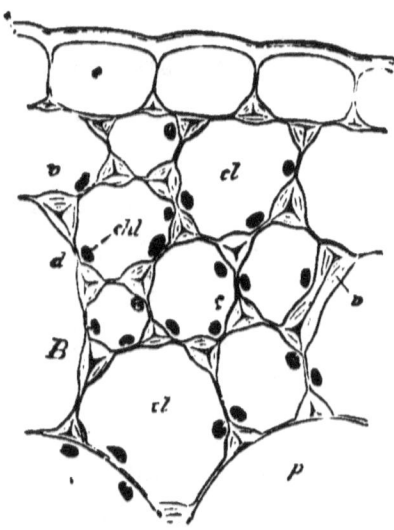

Fig. 151.—Leaf stalk of a Begonia cut across (transverse section). *e*, epidermis; *c*, cuticle (magnified 550 times).

---

* Yet the stigma is not *covered over*, you remember (p. 128), as there is a channel down it into the ovary; and there are the little openings or mouths which are found upon leaves (p. 25).

† From the Greek "*epi*," upon, and "*derma*," skin.

‡ From the Latin (*cutis*), "*cuticula*," the outermost skin.

epidermis soon breaks or bursts as the stem or shoot grows larger, and is changed into, or its place is taken by, the tougher, thicker, and at last hard and brownish tissue, which we commonly call bark, but about which I will tell you a little more in the next chapter.

(3) We come now to an important system or arrangement of tissue, which is made up of both cells and vessels. You have noticed it often in the veins of leaves. These so-called veins are really bundles of tissue, harder than the rest of the substance or tissue of the leaf, and passing from the leaf into and down the branches and main stem like bundles of string or cord. When all the rest of the leaf has perished, these bundles of tissue often remain, and form the skeleton leaves which are so delicately beautiful. If you break a stem of the common plantain leaf, or pull the leaf in two, you will probably see these bundles of tissue projecting very plainly. But you have noticed them also in the fibres of nettles (p. 51); and now I think I can tell you what this combination of cellular and vascular tissue is called. Because its cellular tissue is largely prosenchyma (p. 168), and the cells particularly long, thickened, and tough (fibrous), it is specified by the word *fibro*, and so the combination tissue is known as *fibro-vascular.**

---

* From the Latin "*fibra*," a thread; to mark the thread or string-like character of most of the cells of the cellular tissue. For "vascular," see p. 169.

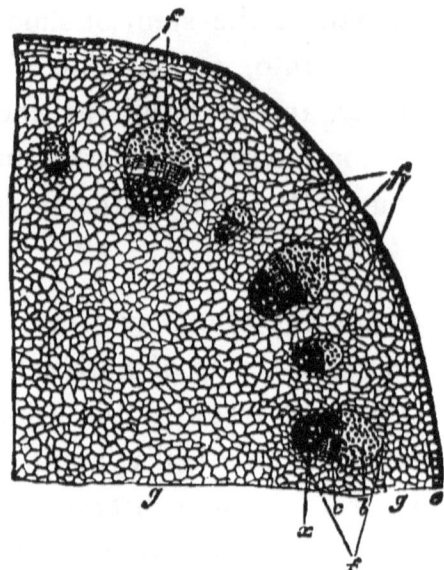

Fig. 152.—Part of leaf stalk of Hellebore (transverse section). *e*, epidermis; *f*, fibro-vascular system; *g*, fundamental tissue.

If you look at the picture of part of a stalk which has been cut across in Fig. 152, you will see the fibro-vascular bundles or tissue very plainly.

(4) All other tissues of which plants are made up, besides the epidermal and the fibro-vascular tissues, are spoken of generally as *fundamental* tissue*. It consists largely of parenchyma (p. 167), and you can find examples of it in the softer parts of leaves and herbaceous stems, in the pith of elder, etc., in the pulp of fruits, in the shell of the walnut, or the stone of the plum or peach.

I hope you will not be disheartened at these three systems or formations of tissue, with their long names coming all together. Think of what the names mean, that you may understand generally what the tissues are. Take another general look at them in Fig. 152, and I will tell you a little more particularly about them when I tell you about wood and bark in another chapter.

---

* From the Latin "*fundamentum*," from "*fundo*," I found, serving for the foundation.

CHAPTER XXX.

WOOD AND BARK.

Fig. 153.—Cuckoo pint (*Arum maculatum*), showing spadix, spathe, and sagittate leaves.

I AM now going to tell you a little more about the fibro-vascular bundles; so let us look at them in a buttercup plant, or in a leafy branch of bush or tree, such as the sycamore or flowering currant. The fibro-vascular bundles which have grown up within the main stem of the herb or tree, have branched out with and within its branches, and you can see them as they branch for the last time and appear as veins in the blades of the leaves.

Now I want you to try and understand the two most common ways in which these fibro-vascular bundles are arranged within the stems. In monocotyledons* they pass up the stem, scattered about here and there in the fundamental tissue (Fig. 154). But in dicotyledons* the bundles

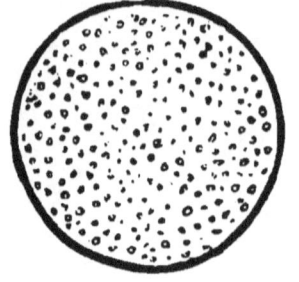

Fig. 154.—Monocotyledonous stem.

are arranged in it so as to form a ring. The pictures will help you to understand this better, as they show you the surfaces of two stems which have been cut across. It is the ringed arrangement which occurs in most of our native trees (Fig. 155). In Fig. 152 you have already noticed the ring of fibro-vascular bundles (*f*) surrounding and surrounded by the fundamental tissue.

Fig. 155.—Section of oak, several years' growth.

But notice the picture, Fig. 152, a little more closely. The bundles you see are made up of a darker and a lighter part. The

---

* From the Greek "*monos*," one : or *dis* (duo), twice, double, and cotyledons (*cf.* pp. 33 and 154). Monocotyledons, plants of which the seeds have one seed-leaf ; dicotyledons, plants of which they have two.

innermost and darker part (*x*) is made up of tissues which become hard in shrubs and trees, and form the *xylem*,* or *wood*. The outer and lighter parts (*cb*) are made up of tissues which are called *phloem*,† or *bast*.

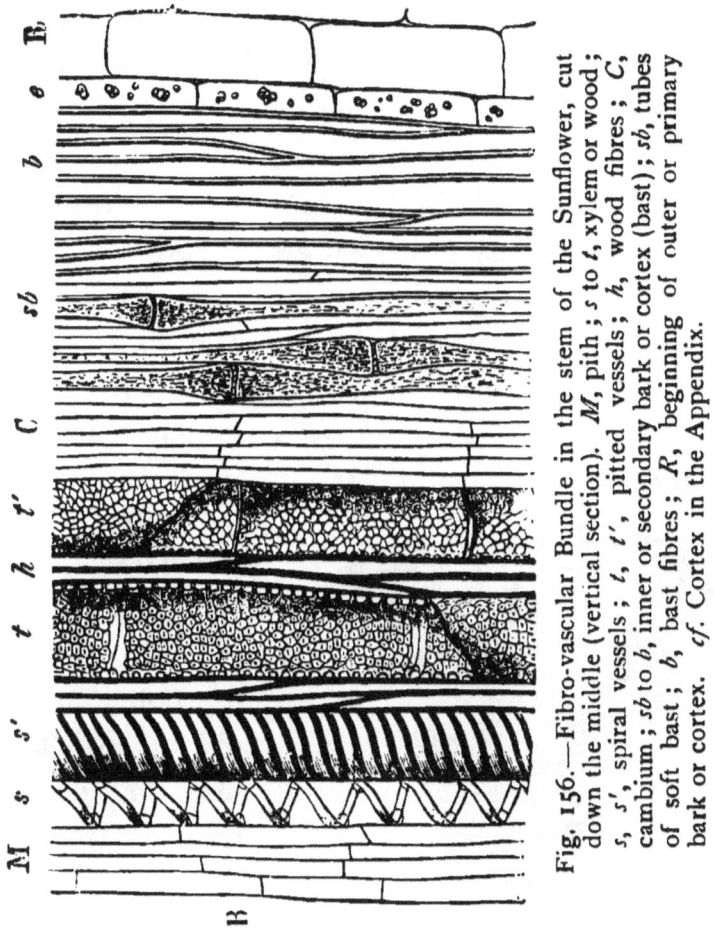

Fig. 156.—Fibro-vascular Bundle in the stem of the Sunflower, cut down the middle (vertical section). *M*, pith; *s* to *t*, xylem or wood; *s, s'*, spiral vessels; *t, t'*, pitted vessels; *h*, wood fibres; *C*, cambium; *sb* to *b*, inner or secondary bark or cortex (bast); *sb*, tubes of soft bast; *b*, bast fibres; *R*, beginning of outer or primary bark or cortex. *cf.* Cortex in the Appendix.

The wood and the bast do not continue to grow, but between them is a set of living and growing cells, called the *cambium*. These cambium cells form new

---

* From the Greek "*xūlon*," wood.
† From the Greek "*phloios*," the inner bark, bast.

tissues year by year, which in their turn cease to grow, and form a permanent addition to the already existing wood and bast bundles, as the case may be. Fig. 156 C shows you the cambium bundles very well.

Now get a small branch of ash or elm, oak, sycamore, or elder, and cut it evenly across. You can easily distinguish the " pith " and the " wood," and the softer part which surrounds the wood, which, I dare say, you call the " bark." Peel off the bark a little. How easily it comes away, and how slippery the wood is where it has been taken off. It is because you have pulled away the bast from the wood, and the cambium cells which lie between them are the growing cells, full of protoplasm, increasing by division, and very tender.

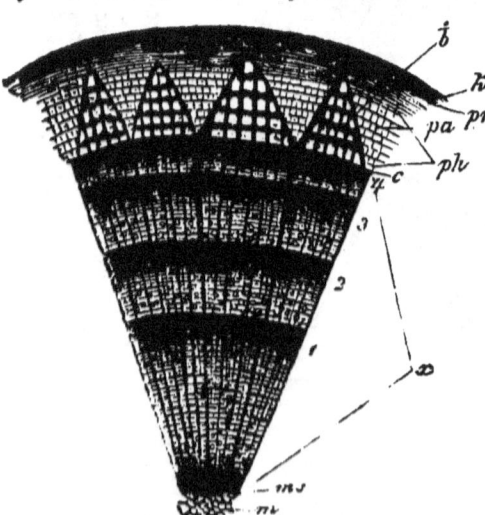

Fig. 157.—Part of a transverse section of a twig of the Lime, four years old. *m*, the pith ; *x*, the wood ; 1, 2, 3, 4, four annual rings ; *c*, cambium ; *ph*, bast ; *b*, bast fibres ; *pr, k*, outer bark.

So now you can understand something about the growth of wood. I do not know how old that little branch may be you have been looking at, so look at Fig. 157. It shows you part of the surface of a four-year-old branch, cut evenly across. Each year the cambium has formed new tissue, more abundantly on its inner side for wood than on its outer side for bast, and the former has hardened year by year into the four rings of wood. This is how it is that in the trunks of many trees you can often plainly see the rings of wood—as many rings as there are years in the age of the tree * (*cf.* Figs. 157, 155).

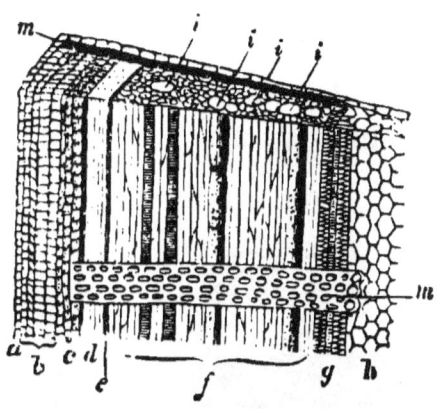

Fig. 158.—Portion of a stem when cut across, showing surface (transverse section) *mi*; and surface when cut lengthwise (longitudinal section) *a* to *h* the pith; *m* shows medullary rays.

In Fig. 158 you can see that there are slits or openings between the fibro-vascular bundles, which go from the cambium towards the pith or medulla. These are called *medullary rays*, and are filled with fundamental tissue (parenchyma). They often add greatly to the beauty of the wood, as for instance in what is known as *silver grain*. In a *transverse* section of a stem, these medullary rays appear as rays from the pith towards the bark (Fig. 157). And compare Figs. 152

---

* Because the new wood is added to the outside of that already formed, stems of this kind of growth (dicotyledons, p. 176) have been called "*exogenous.*" The word is derived from two Greek words "*ex,*" "*exo,*" outwards, on the outside, and "*genō,*" old form of "*gignomai,*" to come into being. The stem increases in thickness by addition upon the outside of the wood only. When the fibro-vascular bundles grow here and there amongst the fundamental tissue irregularly, the plants have been called "*endogenous*" ("*endon,*" within, and "*genō*"). If you cut across a cane, you can see a good example of this growth; and see Fig. 154.

and 159, where the fibro-vascular bundles are some distance apart, showing the fundamental tissue between them, which in an older and more woody stem forms the medullary rays of Fig. 157.

There is much more that is very interesting about the wood, but I must hasten on to tell you a little more about the bark or *cortex*.*

So let us go back to Fig. 157, and take up again the little branch you were looking at just now. In the portion you peeled off from the wood you have those parts of the fibro-vascular bundles which are outside the cambium. Can you tell me what they are called? Yes! they are called "the bast," and they form the *inner* or *secondary bark* or *cortex* (Fig. 157, *ph*, *b*).

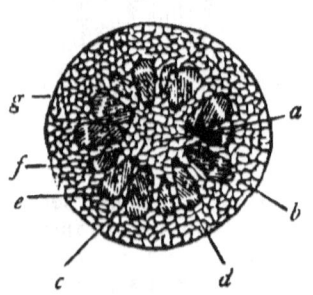

Fig. 159.—Cross section of stem of dicotyledon at end of first year. *a*, pith; *c*, woody tissue, with vessels; *d*, cambium cells; *e*, bast cells; *f g*, outer bark.

Though never hardening into wood, they cease to grow, take a permanent form, and are more or less tough. It is often very useful. I dare say you know it very well as the bast, often from the lime tree, which gardeners use for tying up their plants. So, again, the bast of the hemp and flax plants is so much used for making string and linen,

---

* From the Latin "*cortex*," the rind or bark.

that the name of the whole plant often means only the useful bast which the plant contains.

The *outer bark*, or bark proper (primary cortex), consists mainly of fundamental tissue (Figs. 157 *pr*, 159 *f*). Generally, upon its outside layer, and so just under the epidermis, are formed cells, with walls of cork. This cork cell tissue, through which water hardly penetrates, prevents nourishment from reaching the epidermis of the young

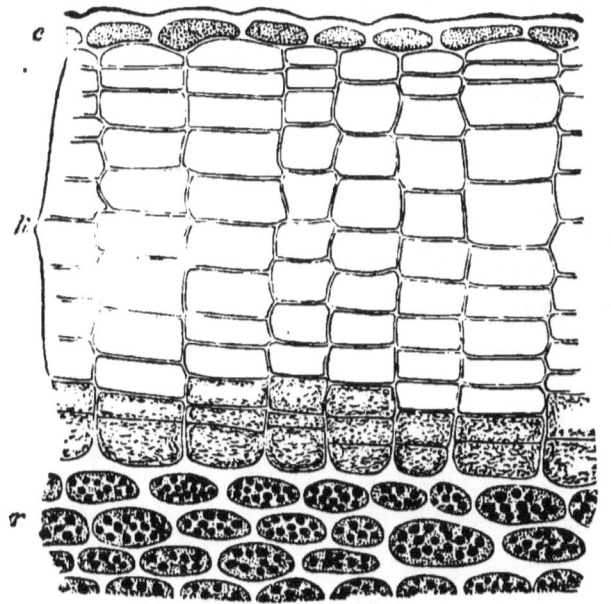

Fig. 160.—Transverse section of a one year's shoot of Ailanthus (foreign), magnified 350 times. *r*, primary cortex; *k*, cork cells; *e*, dead epidermis.

stem, and so towards autumn the once green and living skin becomes brown, and at length it withers and dies away. Its place is taken by the cork tissue, which has caused its death (Figs. 160, 157 *k*). Often the cork tissue grows to a considerable thickness, as in certain kinds of foreign oak, and is very useful when made into bungs and corks, and for many other purposes. But you can tell me now why the outside of the bark is so dry and dead. Yes, it is because the cork cells hinder the passage of the sap, and both the cork and any other tissues that may be outside it become the dry, hard, outside of the bark, or cortex.

Now turn to Fig. 156, and trace again the wood, cambium, bast (making up inner bark), and outer bark; and notice how the latter is continued into the dead outside in Fig. 160.

In roots the fibro-vascular bundles are differently arranged; but this, and other differences of structure between roots and stems, you will search out in time to come.

CHAPTER XXXI.

CONTENTS OF CELLS AND VESSELS.

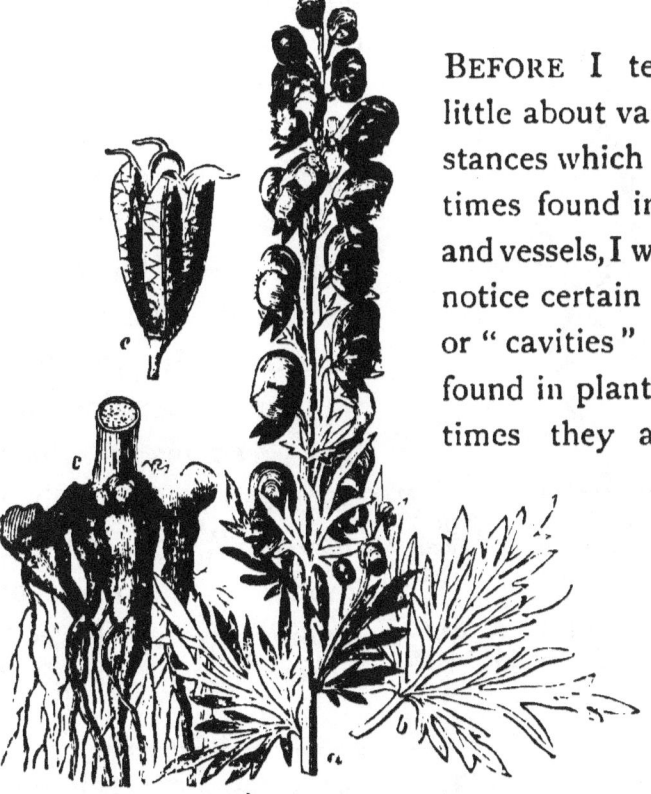

Fig. 161.—Monk's Hood (*Aconitum napellus*). *c*, the root ; *e*, apocarpous fruit (*follicles*).

BEFORE I tell you a little about various substances which are sometimes found in the cells and vessels, I want you to notice certain "spaces" or "cavities" which are found in plants. Sometimes they are found between the cells you remember, and are then called "intercellular spaces" (Fig. 143).

But you can easily see some larger cavities, or *air chambers*. Cut across some part of a large water plant, such as the leaf stalk of a water lily, for instance, and look at it through your magnifying glass; or cut through the hollow stems of the "kecksie," or a grass or rush, some of which you can find quite easily. You will inquire hereafter how these cavities are formed.

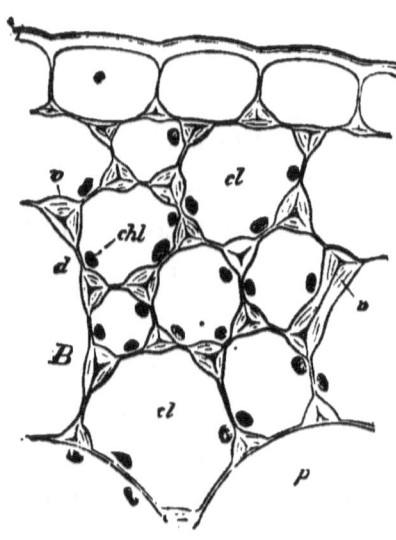

Fig. 162.—Transverse section of leaf stalk of a Begonia. *e*, epidermis; *c*, cuticle; *cl*, a kind of fundamental tissue, with cell walls thickened; *chl*, chlorophyll corpuscles in the cells; *p*, parenchyma cell (magnified 550 times).

Now I am going to tell you about some of the substances which are found sometimes in the intercellular spaces, as well as in vessels or cells.

First, then, about the little green bodies or corpuscles, which are embedded in the protoplasm of certain cells. The green matter which colours them is called *chlorophyll*, so they are known by the name of *chlorophyll corpuscles*.*

It is the presence of

---

* Chlorophyll: from the Greek "*chloros*," green, and "*phullon*," a leaf; because it makes the leaves green. Corpuscle: from the Latin "*corpusculum*," a little body. These chlorophyll corpuscles are portions of separated protoplasm, and are very important to the plant. I will tell you more about them presently.

these little bodies that causes the green colour of so many parts of plants (Fig. 162). But about this, and the presence of other colouring matter in the cells of plants, you must try to learn more particularly after you have read the chapters upon Physiology. Meanwhile, the more you notice the exquisite colours which abound in plants, the rich contrasts of flowers and fruits, so pleasing in their setting of the prevailing and restful green, the more, I think, you will admire them. So, also, our common trees will give you many a beautiful picture in the spring and early summer in the colours of their fresh expanded leaves, and in the autumn if you notice them as their leaves begin to fade and die.

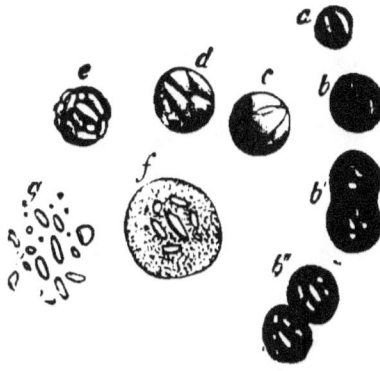

Fig. 163.—Chlorophyll corpuscles with starch grains, from a leaf magnified 550 times. *a, b, c, d, e,* corpuscles of increasing age: in the latter ones the starch fills almost the whole space; *f, g,* after washing and soaking in water, by which the substance of the corpuscle has been destroyed, and only the starchy contents remain; *b' b''* show corpuscle dividing.

Perhaps you have never seen the "starch grains" which are so often found in plant cells, especially those of the potato tubers, beans, or wheat or rice, and kindred seeds (Fig. 163). If you take a bit of potato tuber, and well soak it, soften, separate, and wash it in water, you will presently have a little white powder remaining. Look at it through your magnifying glass. Under the microscope you could see the starch granules very plainly. Sometimes the shape of them is very strange (Fig. 164). These starch granules make the tubers, or seeds which contain them, very nutritious as food. Sugar is found in the cell sap of the sugar cane, the beetroot, and some other plants.

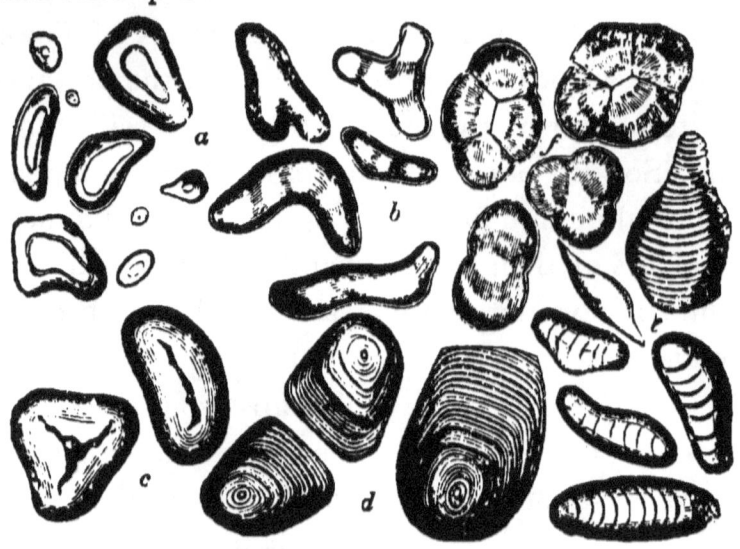

Fig. 164.—Starch Grains.

Hard "crystals" are also found in the cells of plants. Here is a picture of some of them (Fig. 166), but you may easily find some real ones. Take a hyacinth stem, break or cut it, and rub the cut part gently along a glass slide; now if you look through your magnifying glass you will very likely be able to see some of the crystals like tiny needles (Fig. 166). Crystals of this shape

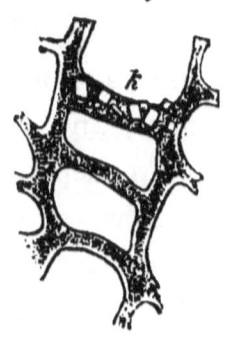

Fig. 165.—Crystals in the wall of some cell tissue, magnified six hundred times.

are called "*raphides.*"* You would find crystals of another shape in the stalks of rhubarb.

Now we will pick a dandelion, and notice its milky juice. It is contained in vessels, long tubes or ducts, which spread thickly both in root and flower stalk. Common sun's purge also has a quantity of milky juice which is contained in cells, and is white in colour as in the dandelion. But do you know the greater celandine? † It is a plant with little clusters of yellow flowers, each of four petals, and its seed vessel is a pod; it grows in waste places, thickets, and often about old houses. Its abundant milky juice is yellow.

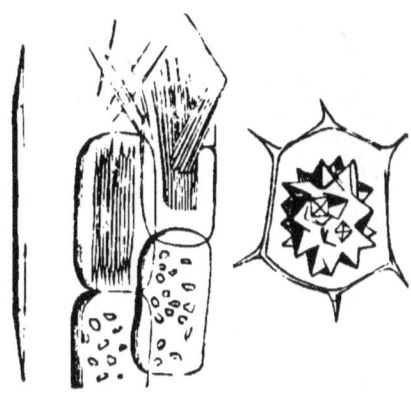

Fig. 166.—Crystals and Raphides.

In some plants this kind of milky juice is very valuable. Opium for instance is the milky juice which is found in the capsules of a certain kind of poppy, ‡ and the milky juice of a foreign § plant, of the same natural order as our common

---

* From the Greek "*raphis,*" a needle.

† Not the buttercup celandine (*Ficaria verna*), but quite a different plant, the *Chelidonium majus*.

‡ *Papaver somniferum.*

§ *Siphonia elastica.*

Fig. 167.—Corner of leaf of Scotch fir, showing resin ducts.

spurge, becomes, when it is dried, our india rubber.

I daresay you have often noticed the "gum" upon the plum or cherry trees, or the "resinous" substance upon the firs (Fig. 167). These are formed in the cells, vessels, and inter-cellular spaces of various parts of the plants in which they are produced; as also the oil or scent which you find so pleasant when you bruise a myrtle leaf, or bend and squeeze the rind of an orange or lemon * (Fig. 168).

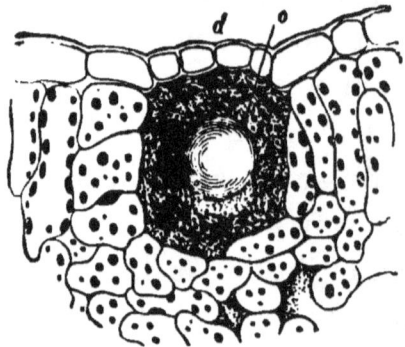

Fig. 168.—Oil cavity with drop of volatile oil (*o*), from below the upper surface of a leaf of *Dictamnus* (foreign), magnified 320 times.

You see how much there is for you to enquire about and examine, not only concerning the way plants are made up, but also as to the substances which they contain.

But we must pass on to the way in which plants live and grow. So I shall conclude our talks upon the anatomy of plants by telling you about the beautiful bloom which you often see upon our choicest fruits. What is the "bloom," and what is it for?

---

* Notice the leaves of the St. John's wort (*Hypericum perforatum*), which have these oil cavities; they appear like transparent dots or spots.

It is a kind of wax which is in the cuticle (p. 172) of many plants, and which sometimes forms a covering or bloom of very minute particles upon the surface of the fruit, to protect it from being damaged by the rain.

PHYSIOLOGY.

CHAPTER XXXII.

ABSORPTION AND TRANSPIRATION.

Fig. 169.—Lily of the Valley (*Convallaria majalis*). *d*, stamens with open anthers, showing pollen; *f*, trilocular capsule; *g*, transverse section.

In the first beginning of life there is a mystery which cannot be explained; so at present you must be content to know that under certain conditions of warmth and moisture the little cells of a seed begin to move and grow, and the seed is found to be alive.

But I think you will be able to tell me what the

little plant or embryo lives upon until it has burst its seed coat, and settled itself in the world to enjoy plant life as its parents did before it. Yes, until its plumule becomes a stem, and its radicle a root, so that it can take its own food from soil and atmosphere, it feeds upon the store food with which its thoughtful parent has supplied it, from endosperm, or perisperm, or cotyledon store as the case may be (p. 154). You can easily notice the testa of the wheat or bean seed becoming more and more empty and withered as the little plantlet grows.

You can see the same kind of thing also in the tuber of the potato or the orchis, as the young buds grow and live upon the treasured food.

So now we have come to the young plant, fairly started and continuing to grow according to the methods and laws of plant life, about which I am going to tell you.

What then is the food of plants? In the first place, it is composed of certain gases, such as oxygen and nitrogen, and of certain solids, such as sulphur and iron, which are mixed up with a great deal of water into liquid food. For plants take up food by their roots from the earth in which they grow, and the roots can only take it in a liquid form. Now let us pull up some common plant and look at the thinner fibres of its root; with a magnifying glass you can sometimes see their root hairs (p. 73) growing from the epidermal cells; and notice also how particles of soil stick to them—they are taking up from the ground their liquid food. In transplanting plants, therefore, you should be careful to injure as little as possible the ends and finer portions of their roots. This taking up by the roots of liquid food is called "*absorption*."

Now what becomes of this liquid food, or sap as it is called? It ascends from cell to cell, and from vessel to vessel, passing through their thin walls up through the stem and branches to the leaves.[*] But the plant takes in largely through the leaves some more food, which it absorbs from the atmosphere. Great changes take place, and the sap with new matter in it passes down again through cells and vessels, forming new substances as it goes, and helping the plant to grow.

When you know more about chemistry, you will be able to learn particularly what these changes are which take place in the sap and substance of the plant. I will only try and give you a general idea of the means by which they are brought about.

One of them is the getting rid of some of the water of the sap. This takes place by evaporation from those parts of plants which are exposed to the air, and is called "*transpiration*."[†] The water, in the form of vapour, is breathed out or given off into the

---

[*] *cf. diffusion* in the Appendix.
[†] From the Latin "*trans*," across, and "*spiro*," I breathe.

atmosphere through the thin walls of any cells where it is not prevented by the cuticle (p. 172).

Now, if you take the epidermis of some common land plant, and examine it under the microscope, you will find dotted here and there upon most parts of it, especially upon the leaves, the little openings, which are called *stomates* or *stomata*.* Here is a picture of part of the surface of a leaf, very much magnified, which shows a few of them (Fig. 170); but they are very numerous, and are found chiefly on the under sides of leaves.† The stomate is generally formed of two sausage or kidney-shaped cells placed together with the hollowed (concave) sides facing each other, and so having a little opening between them as in Fig. 170. But the opening between them varies according as the cells are more or less swollen with sap; and the stomate is also much

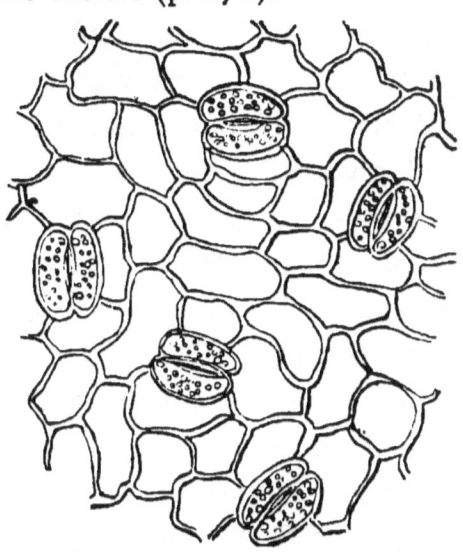

Fig. 170.—Epidermis of leaf showing stomata (highly magnified). *cf.* Figs. 20, 21, p. 25.

---

* From the Greek "*stoma*," a mouth : plural "*stomata.*"

† Botanists have calculated that there are more than 100,000 stomata upon an ordinary sized apple leaf, and more than half a million upon a leaf of the common lilac.

In water plants the stomates are usually wanting in parts under water, and are upon the upper surfaces of floating leaves. There are no stomates upon roots.

influenced by the light to which it is exposed, as well as by the dryness or dampness of the atmosphere. Through the stomates transpiration can readily take place, and it is often very considerable. It has been calculated that a common sunflower, $3\frac{1}{2}$ feet high, will give off a quart of fluid in a single day.

I dare say you have noticed the leaves drooping upon transplanted plants, and that in times of heat and drought some plants begin to droop much sooner than others. These are caused by the transpiration of fluid through the leaves more quickly than a fresh supply can be taken up through the roots.

You will perhaps understand the action of the stomata better if you look at Fig. 171. There you can see what the substance or thickness of a beech leaf is like. It is cut in two, and held so that you look at the cut edge very much magnified. You see how the stomate opens into a space or air cavity, and so the surrounding cells of the parenchyma are open to the atmosphere, and transpiration can easily take place.

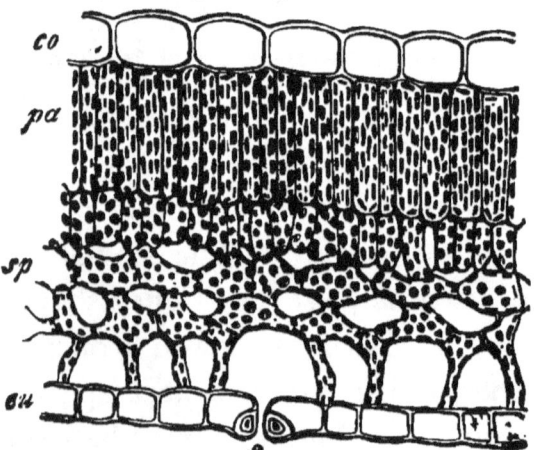

Fig. 171.—Transverse section of a beech leaf (magnified 350 times); *co*, epidermis of upper surface; *eu*, epidermis of under surface; *pa*, parenchyma; *sp*, parenchyma with cavities; *s*, a stoma.

CHAPTER XXXIII.

FURTHER CHANGES IN THE SAP.

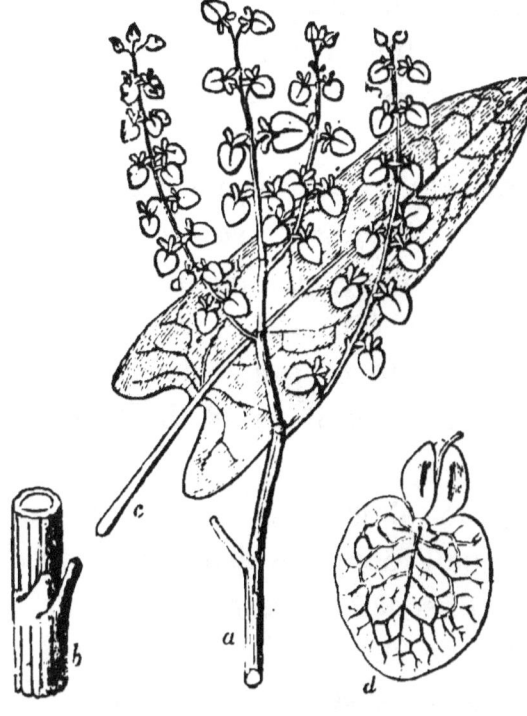

Fig. 172.—Inflorescence and leaf of Dock (*Rumex*); *d*, magnified petal.

WE will provide ourselves with a common pickle jar, and about an inch of a small candle or wax-taper bound on to a bit of wire a little longer than the jar, and bend the wire so that you can easily hold the candle inside and close to the bottom of the jar.

So now I will tell you a little about what takes place when the plant takes in its food from the atmosphere (p. 192). There is a gas in the atmosphere which is called *carbonic acid gas*, or *carbon dioxide*, and as I want you to remember it, I will show you what a deadly gas it sometimes is. So we will light our bit of candle. Now you shall lower it down into the jar; and I will hold the cork upon the jar's mouth to close it. At first the candle burns all right, but soon it grows dim and then, yes, now you see it has gone out. Why is that? The burning candle has used up the good air of the atmosphere upon which its flame could burn or live, and the kind of air of which the jar is now full is a gas in which the candle cannot burn any more. Let us take the candle out, and light it, and see if this is really so. Yes, as soon as you lower the candle into the jar it goes out. Now you and I every moment we live are using up the good air of the atmosphere, just like the burning candle did in the pickle jar, and breathing out instead of it the other kind of gas which will not support our life any more than it would the flame of the candle.

Have you ever read about the Black Hole of Calcutta? It was a small room in which one hundred and forty-six British prisoners were shut up by the Sepoys during the Indian Conquest. It was so small that they were terribly crowded, and when the doors were opened in the morning only twenty-three of all the one hundred and forty-six were still alive. They had been breathing in the good air, and breathing out the bad gas, until the atmosphere became such that it would hardly support life any longer; so almost all of them died, like the candle flame went out just now within the pickle jar. If they had been left a little longer the rest would have died also. What a wonder that with so many people in the world, the air does not all get spoilt, like it did in the Black Hole of Calcutta.

But that bad kind of gas which is always being produced by men and animals, and in some other ways also, as you have seen by the burning candle, is just what the plants want. Under the influence of sun light they take it in, use up and live upon a part of it, and give back another part of it to the atmosphere again to make it pure and ready for our use. For this carbonic acid gas,* so deadly to us, which the plant takes in from the atmosphere, comes in contact with those little green bodies which I told you are found in certain cells, which are called chlorophyll corpuscles (p. 184). Then, but only under the influence of light, the gas and the corpuscle both become changed. The gas is broken up; part of it (oxygen gas) which makes the atmosphere pure and good for us to breathe again, is sent back again to do that useful work. Part of it (carbon) joins with the substance of the corpuscle, and so, as a general rule, forms little grains of starch. This work, or process, is called *assimilation*,† because the plant takes in what it wants from the atmosphere (carbon), and makes it part of itself, for the starch grains are the

---

* *cf.* Appendix, "*atmosphere*," "*carbonic acid gas.*"

† From the Latin "*assimilo*," I make like. The act of converting something into its own substance. *cf. carbon* in the Appendix.

great stores from which the plant builds up its substance.

But whilst assimilation goes on only under the influence of light, always by day and by night plants are working in another way in connection with the air. They are taking in the oxygen and giving off carbonic acid gas, and this is known by the name of *respiration*.* What a good thing it is that plant-respiration, by which the plants take up that part of the air which we require to live upon and give off that gas upon which we cannot live, is very small compared with plant assimilation, which does the very contrary; so small that on the whole it is not noticeable, and does not hinder the great and beneficial work which the plants do for us by assimilation.

So if you have many flowers in your room during the dark hours of night, when no assimilation is going on, but respiration continues, they will help to make the air impure and unhealthy for you. Indeed flowers which are not green (p. 197) do not assimilate at all, but they respire the carbonic acid gas; and some are particularly injurious, because of other poisons which they give off.

So now by these changes the liquid food or sap has become much changed from what it was when first absorbed by the roots (crude sap). It has been added to and altered, mainly in the leaves, and as it

---

* From the Latin "*re*," again, and "*spiro*," I breathe. To breathe out again, to breathe back.

moves away from the chlorophyll corpuscles the starch grains or carbon food (p. 197) mixed up or dissolved in it are carried with it. Thus, as it passes through certain cells and vessels through the plant, the food taken up in liquid form from the earth and in gaseous form from the atmosphere all works in together; and new substances are formed or old ones added to as the case may be. These further changes are called by one name, "*metastasis.*"* In this way the protoplasm of plants is nourished, and so the living cells and vessels of plants increase and cause the tissues, that is the plant, to grow. In this way are formed the solid crystals, as well as starch and oils and other things, about some of which I told you in the last chapter.

In this way food is stored up in certain parts of plants for future use. Easy examples of this are found in tubers, tubercles, rhizomes, bulbs, and seeds. They contain, as you know, stores of food ready to support the growth of the young plant until by its own roots and other organs it can take in fresh food to supply its daily need.

Now what I want you to remember is that plants can feed upon elementary substances, which you and I and animals cannot do. Carbon, for instance, is an elementary substance—that is chemists cannot separate

---

* From the Greek "*meta*," over, and "*stasis*," a placing or setting (fr : "*histēmi*," I stand). A removal or alteration. It is also called "*metabolism.*"

it into two different parts ; and it is necessary to life. But we cannot take it alone—we can only take it when it is combined with other substances. We must have prepared food. Now this is just what the plants do for us. As we have seen, they take in the carbon and assimilate or combine it into their own substance. Then in this combined and prepared form you and I and the animals in general can use the stalks, leaves, seeds, and other parts of plants as food.

How wonderful is this and of what vital importance to us are the plants! Silently, but busily, they are working for us all the day long, not only purifying the atmosphere for us to breathe, but also actually preparing food for us to eat. Under God's Providence, through the working of the plants, we can breathe and eat and live.

CHAPTER XXXIV.

GROWING PLANTS.

Fig. 173.—Acacia. With bipinnate leaves and lomentaceous fruit.

You will now, I hope, understand a little about the way in which plants live and grow. First, you will remember that their food is made up of solids, liquids, and gases; but the solids are dissolved, as plants can only take up their food in a liquid or a gaseous form—*absorption* (p 192). Then, whilst superfluous fluid is got rid of by *transpiration* (p. 192), carbon is obtained by *assimilation* (p. 197), oxygen is taken in by *respiration* (p. 198), new tissues and other substances are formed by *metastasis*, and so the plant lives and grows.*

I want you to like this part of botany, and so I will try to show you further how many interesting things there are connected with it and how very useful this kind of knowledge is.

Suppose, for instance, that we consider some of those things without which plants cannot live; and if I repeat anything that I have already told you it will help you to remember it. We will take light, heat, air, earthy food and water.

Would it not be terrible if our herbs and leaves were all white instead of green. But that is just what happens when plants grow without any light. I daresay you have noticed this in sprouts of potatoes which have been kept in darkness, or in the white stems of sea-kale, or the celery stem so beautifully white where it was covered by the earth, whilst its top which was exposed to the light is of the familiar green. Without light no green chlorophyll is formed and we should lose the beautiful green colouring so restful to our eyes. Without light no carbon would be

---

* *cf. parasite* in the Appendix.

assimilated and the plants would die, and we, too, should perish for want of food.

Then I expect you have noticed how long and thin the white shoots of the potatoes are when they have been stored in a dark place, that is because light affects the rapidity of growth; it checks it and prevents the plant growing too fast. The white weak potato shoots grow unhealthily and too fast for want of light. This helps us to understand why plants placed in a window bend towards the light, the side of the stem away from the light grows faster than the side which is towards it, and so the stem becomes curved over upon its shortest side, that is towards the light. You see that in a healthy plant just as in a healthy boy or girl all the processes or movements of life must go on in proper degree.

So also plants are greatly affected by changes in the temperature or heat of the atmosphere. The heat which will suit some will destroy others, so the "flora" or flowering plant life is different in countries or districts according to their heat or cold. Some plants which do very well in a greenhouse, or sheltered south border of your garden, will not thrive in more exposed and colder places, so that with the plants in frames and green-houses gardeners are always careful about the heat as well as about the light they give to them. You will understand that this is the more necessary when you remember about transpiration, and because of assimilation and respiration you will understand why the plant needs a proper supply of air.

In wild places the herbs and leaves of trees decay upon the ground where they grow and so give back to the earth what they took away from it by their roots. But if the crops are taken away from the land and nothing put into it again it gradually gets poorer and poorer until at last there is not enough food in it for the plants to thrive upon. This is why the manuring of land is so necessary, and it requires both knowledge and judgment to give the land that kind of manure or food which will best suit the kind of plant which we are about to grow.

Then from a knowledge of the nature of plants as to their need with regard to water has grown up the science of draining.

But I have said enough to show you that without some knowledge of the physiology of plants, farmers and gardeners and those who have to do with the life and growth of plants, cannot work intelligently, and can hardly expect to be successful.

We will end our talks on physiology by my telling you about the length of time plants live. Some only have one flowering season and then die. These are called "*monocarpous*,"* one fruiting. A few of them

---

* From the Greek "*monos*," one ; or "*polŭs*," many ; and "*karpos*," fruit.

live some years before they blossom, fruit, and die. But generally these monocarpous plants spring up, produce seed and die in a single year, when they are called "*annuals*,"† as wheat: or they do not come into flower and seed until the second year and then die, as the turnip; these are called "*biennials.*" †

But many plants blossom and seed continually year after year and so are called *polycarpous.** These are shrubs and trees with woody stems and herbs with underground stems, such as rhizomes, bulbs, etc. These are commonly called "*perennials.*"†

How long do seeds keep alive? They vary very much, but some will grow after very many years if the life has not been destroyed by heat or cold or other special cause. Dr. Hooker mentioned an instance of an Indian bean growing after 100 years as being one of the longest proved instances of seed life; but this is a very much disputed point. If, however, you are ever near a place where new soil has been thrown up to the surface, as in a gravel pit or railway cutting, always look for any new plant, new to the neighbourhood at least, which may have sprung up from long buried seed.

So now I hope you know a little about the methods

---

* See note * on page 204.

† From the Latin "*annus*," a year (annual, of one year); "*bis*," twice and *annus* (biennial, of two years); or "*per*," through, and *annus* (perennial, through or during several years).

and laws of plant life about which I have been telling you (physiology). Telling you only a very little, but enough I hope for you to be eager to know more, and able also to take up one of the more advanced books without being easily disheartened by its difficulties.

CLASSIFICATION.

CHAPTER XXXV.

CLASSES.

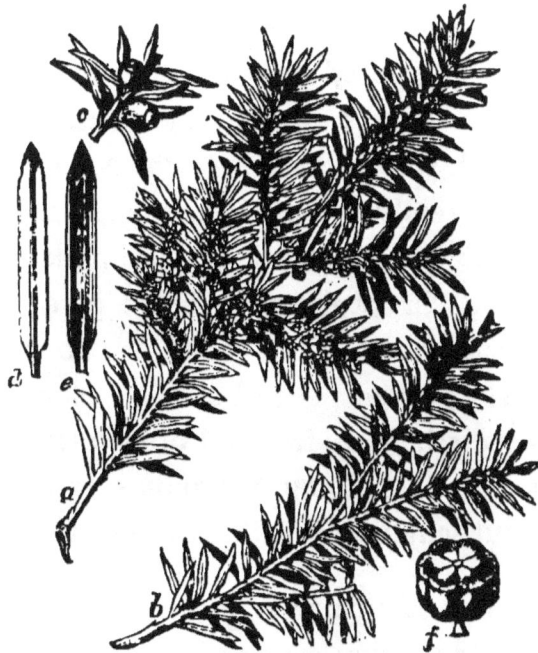

Fig. 174.—Yew. (*Taxus baccata*). *d* leaves. *c* fruit with arillus *f.*

You will remember, I hope, that the plant kingdom is made up of two great divisions or sub-kingdoms: (1) the "flowering," (2) the "flowerless" plants (p. 10). The flowerless plants, fungi, and seaweeds, and lichens, and mosses, and ferns, you will learn about at some future time if you wish to do so. I will only tell you now that the flowerless plants are called *Cryptogams*. They are so called because they have no flowers such as you have been learning about in "Flower-land," and so the way in which they are reproduced is comparatively "hidden." The flowering plants on the other hand, are called *Phanerogams* or *Phænogams*, because the flowers and their parts producing seeds, from which young plants grow up again, are plainly "seen."*

But I must now tell you that some of the plants I have spoken of as flowerless have flower-like organs, only they do not produce seed. A seed, you remember, is a young plant, of course very tiny and not developed, but still there—root, stem, and leaves in their beginnings and all enclosed in a skin or covering. It is the production of seeds by which the plants of this sub-kingdom, which we have called Phænogams or flowering plants, are really to be distinguished and separated from the plants of that other sub-kingdom which we have called Cryptogams. These plants, therefore, which you have been learning about are most accurately called seed-bearing plants or *Spermaphytes*† in distinction from all other plants which do not bear seeds. They reproduce themselves by spores, about which you will learn hereafter.

Now I want you particularly to notice one or two things so that you may be able to

---

* The words are taken from the Greek. *Cryptogam*, the manner of production, "*kruptos*," *i.e.* hidden. *Phanerogam*, the manner of production, "*phaneros*," *i.e.* visible.

† From the Greek "*sperma*," a seed, and "*phutos*," "*phuo*," to bring forth, to produce.

distinguish from one another the three classes into which Spermaphytes are divided.

1. Are there any yew trees in your neighbourhood? They are diœcious, you know (p. 123), and I want you to find some of the pistil bearing trees. They will be in flower in April, but later in the season will be all the better for you. Then you will see the little green seeds, each with its greenish cup in which it is fixed something like an egg in an egg cup. Gradually the greenish cup thickens and becomes juicy and red. It is called an "*arillus*" (Fig. 174). You have often seen them, I dare say, and very pretty they are.

But what I want you to notice is not the cup or arillus, but the seed which it partly surrounds. I want you to remember that it is a seed, and not like the acorn or nut, a seed enclosed in an ovary. For instance, if you pick some common flower of good size, primrose or poppy or hyacinth, one of which the corolla has faded away, one which has "gone to seed." Where is the seed? Quite right. It is ripening within the ovary; cut open the ovary and there you can see the seed. You can see the seed of the yew quite well without cutting or disturbing anything. The ovules of the yew were not enclosed in ovaries, and when they were fertilized (p. 133), ripened as uncovered or naked seeds. So plants of this habit are called *gymnosperms*,* because their seeds are

---

* See note * on next page.

uncovered and naked ; whilst plants like the primrose are called *angiosperms*,* because their seeds are enclosed within an ovary.

This is one of the characteristic differences which you should remember, so that you may be able to distinguish from one another the " classes " into which spermaphytes have been divided.

2. The next difference is also connected with the seed. It has to do with the number of the cotyledons of the embryo, about which I have already told you (p. 154). And you know that when the embryo of the seed has only one cotyledon (p. 176) the plant is called a *monocotyledon* ; when it has two opposite cotyledons the plant is called a dicotyledon. But when the seed has more than two cotyledons (some of the gymnosperms have as many as fifteen) the plant is called a *polycotyledon*.

So far then we have the three classes of Phænogams arranged as follows :—

    Class I. Angiosperms and Dicotyledons.
    Class II. Angiosperms and Monocotyledons.
    Class III. Gymnosperms and Dicotyledons or Polycotyledons.

But these differences are not always easy for you to see. So I will mention some other differences which you can observe more easily.

---

* From the Greek "*aggos*," "*aggeion*," a vessel, or "*gumnos*," naked, and "*sperma*," seed.

3. You must notice the venation of the leaves, whether they are straight-veined or net-veined leaves (p. 35).

4. So also the shape of the leaves, whether they are simple or compound, whether they are entire or notched.

5. Then as to the structure and manner of growth of the stem. Sometimes it is such as I have described in chapter XXX. (Fig. 155, p. 176). This kind of stem you remember has been called *exogenous*, and so a plant with such a stem has been called an *exogens* (p. 179).

But sometimes the fibro-vascular bundles are scattered here and there amidst the fundamental tissue. The stem when cut across shows no regular rings, the fibro-vascular bundles growing wherever within the stem they may happen to be (Fig. 154, p. 176). So this kind of stem has been called *endogenous*; and a plant with such a stem is called an *endogens* (p. 179).

6. Then lastly you may notice the number of the sepals, petals, and stamens of a plant whether they occur in sets of three, or four, or five, etc.

But remember that though any one of these differences is generally a guide to the class to which a plant belongs, it is not so *always*. So when you examine a plant, consider as far as you can all the marks which I have mentioned, and then judge the plant to belong to that class with the characteristics of which it most generally agrees. If you remember this, and study well the table which I now give you, you will seldom fail, I think, to place a British plant in its proper class.

CLASS I.

SEEDS.	LEAVES.	STEM.	PARTS OF FLOWER.
Angiosperms and Dicotyledons.	...Net-veined; in shape & margin various.	...Exogenous	...Four or five or multiple of five, seldom three or multiple of three.*

CLASS II.

Angiosperms and Monocotyledons.	...Straight-veined, shape simple, margin entire.	...Endogenous	...Three or multiple of three, seldom four, never five or multiple of five.

CLASS III.

Gymnosperms and Dicotyledons or Polycotyledons.

The British plants which belong to this class include the pines and firs. The common juniper is one of them, and so, as we have seen (p. 209) is the common yew. Their leaves are simple and entire.

---

* Multiple: A number into which the other number can be divided without any remainder. Thus, six and nine are multiples of three; en is a multiple of five.

CHAPTER XXXVI.

FROM CLASS TO NATURAL ORDER.

Fig. 175.—Coltsfoot. (*Tussilago farfara*). *c* top of flower stalk, showing reflexed involucre, receptacle and florets. *d* single floret (magnified), of the margin, ligulate. *e* single floret of the disk, tubular (magnified.)

You will now be able, I think, to find out to which of the three classes a plant belongs. Next you want to find its "*natural order*." But as there are about a hundred natural orders (British), it is not always easy to find out to which of them your plant belongs.

So to help you, botanists divide the classes into sub-classes and divisions, different writers doing so upon different plans. You will be able to understand and use these classifications if you remember what I have told you in the chapters on morphology, with one or two additions, which I will now give you.

So let us see if we can find a buttercup. I want you to notice the position of the ovaries relatively to that of the stamens, the corollas, and the calyx. You see the ovaries are superior (p. 118) right at the top of the flower stalk. If you pull off the stamens, petals, and sepals, you take them from the stalk below the ovaries of the pistil (Fig. 176). So because the other parts of the flower are inserted under the pistil, a flower of this kind is called "*hypogynous*"* (Fig. 177, H).

Fig. 176.—Buttercup flower, calyx, corolla, and stamens removed; *f* ovaries, *a* stamens, *s* peduncle, *x* receptacle.

But often it is not so, and then the flower is either "perigynous" or "epigynous." It is "*perigynous*"* when the other floral parts are inserted upon the receptacle or extended axis of the flower-stalk so as to be around but not under

---

* From the Greek "*hupo*," under; "*peri*," around; "*epi*," upon the ovary. These terms are also applied to stamens and petals to describe their insertion.

the ovary (Fig. 177, P). Try examples of this in the bramble, and common avens or herb bennet.

But sometimes when the rim of the flower-stalk is extended far upwards, or a calyx tube far downwards, around the ovary, the calyx, corolla, and stamens, as the case may be, appear as if they were inserted upon the top of the ovary. In this case the ovary is

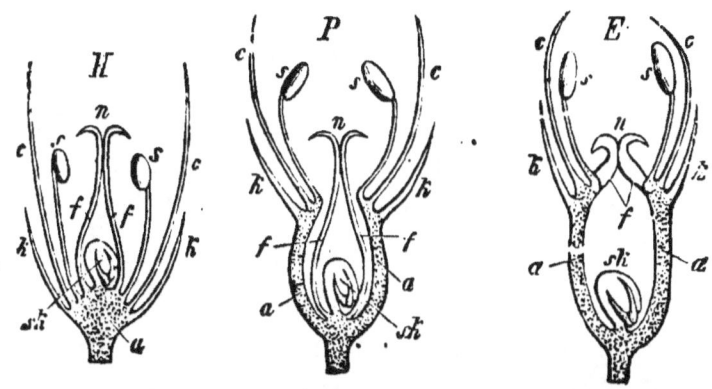

Fig. 177.—*H* Hypogynous. *P* Perigynous. *E* Epigynous. *a* top of stem or axis. *k* calyx. *c* corolla. *s* stamens. *f* carpels. *n* stigma. *sk* ovule.

"inferior" (p 118), and the flower is said to be "*epigynous*,"* as in the carrot, cow-parsnip, or vegetable marrow (Fig. 177 E).

The following terms are also used to mark the various positions of the stamens. A flower is—

Thalamifloral when they spring from the flower-stalk below the ovary (stamens hypogynous).

Discifloral when they are inserted upon the expanded top or disc of the flower-stalk (stamens perigynous).

---

* See note * on page 214.

Calycifloral when they are upon the calyx (stamens perigynous or epigynous).

Corollifloral or *Epipetalous* when they are upon the corolla.

Gynandrous when they are upon the pistil.*

But sometimes these differences are difficult to distinguish, and it may sometimes help you to trace a plant from its class to its natural order if you use the artificial system of classification.

And now you want to know what this artificial system is? Well, the system of classification which I have been hitherto telling you about is called the " natural system." It is so called because plants are arranged in it according to their natural similarities. Other systems have been made which are called artificial. They are so called because plants are grouped together in them which are alike in some special features, but which are often very unlike each other in their general natural characteristics. The artificial system I shall tell you of is the one which was made by the great Swedish botanist Linnæus, and so it is generally called the Linnæan system.

In this plants are grouped in twenty-four classes, the spermaphytes into twenty-three of them, the twenty-fourth including all the other plants. These twenty-three classes are arranged according to the numbers and position of the stamens. If you

---

* *cf. gynous, androus,* in the Appendix.

get "Withering's Handbook to the Linnæan System," I think you will find it useful. It will often help you to make out a plant with which you may be puzzled, as the stamens and pistil are generally easy to examine. The descriptions also of the plants are full. Remember, however, that the natural system is the best and the most interesting, and that is the one which you must take pains to learn and which you should generally use. So we leave the artificial system. For what I want you now to remember is the main framework of the natural system. The classes, the natural orders, the genera, and the species. Then in due course with a book in which plants are described, arranged, and named (a flora)—you will be able to take a plant and find out first the class to which it belongs, then its natural order, then its genus, then its species, and so you will find its general description and its name.

For you remember, I hope, what I told you about the names of plants. Every plant has two names, one its generic or family name, the other its specific or individual name, by which the members of the family are distinguished from one another (Ch. XI.) Now you know that in English we put the individual name first, and the family name second; we say Red Clover to distinguish it from White Clover, just as we say John Brown, to distinguish him from Robert Brown. But the scientific names of plants are in Latin, and then the family or generic name comes first, and the individual or specific name comes second. So instead of the sweet violet its Latin name is *Viola odorata* (violet sweet).

You should take pains to know well at least the three classes (p. 212), so that you can tell to which of them a plant belongs. And you should know also the five natural orders, the cruciferæ (p. 37), the papilionaceæ (leguminosæ, p. 39, 108); the labiatæ (p 42), the umbelliferæ (p. 43, 45), the compositæ (p. 48, 229). You will soon know more as you practise with some British Flora.

I hope also soon to offer you a little handbook, easily carried in your pocket, and useful to help you in finding quickly the names of the plants you meet with in your country rambles.* You could afterwards notice and compare them more fully with your larger flora at home.

I have so much enjoyed our talks and rambles, that I feel to have grown quite at home with you, and loath to say good-bye. You will, however, now be able to take up a more advanced manual of Botany, several very satisfactory ones are published. If you would like to read another small book first, one which I strongly advise you to read is Dr. Hooker's Botany, published by Macmillan & Co., price. 1/- : one of the " Science Primers." Then for your advanced Guide I should advise you to get "An Elementary Text Book

---

* " Who's Who in Flower-Land."

of Botany," by Dr. K. Prantl : edited by Professor S. H. Vines (published by Swan, Sonnenchein & Co.) And I trust that, though apart, we shall still delight in the life and growth of plants, searching out their wonderful works for the benefit and enjoyment of man.

I think there is reason for my repeating my hope that as we gain this greater knowledge, we shall grow in reverence and gratitude towards God, Who is the great Creator and Preserver of all things, and our Heavenly Father.

As you are fond of flowers, read these few verses which I love. It shall be our good-bye, and they will help us to find high and soul-ennobling thoughts as we enjoy the wonders and the beauties which abound in Flower-Land.

    Your voiceless lips, O flowers, are living preachers,
    Each cup a pulpit, every leaf a book,
    Supplying to my fancy numerous teachers
        From loneliest nook.

    'Neath cloistered boughs each floral bell that swingeth,
    And tolls its perfume on the passing air,
    Makes Sabbath in the fields, and ever ringeth
        A call to prayer.

    Not to the domes where crumbling arch and column
    Attest the feebleness of mortal hand,
    But to that fane most catholic and solemn
        Which God hath planned;

To that cathedral, boundless as our wonder,
Whose quenchless lamps the sun and moon supply—
Its choir the winds and waves—its organ thunder—
    Its dome the sky.

There, amid solitude and shade, I wander
Through the green aisles, and, stretched upon the sod,
Awed by the silence, reverently ponder
    The ways of God.

HORACE SMITH.

APPENDIX A.—(General).

Androus.—Used in composition with other words, and refers to the stamens. It is from the Greek "*anēr*," gen. *andros*, a man : the stamens being spoken of as "the men."

(i.) So all the stamens of a flower together are called by one word, the *Andrœcium*; from *andros*, as above, and *oikion*, a house; the man's house.

(ii.) So "androus" is placed as a termination in forming words to tell the number of the stamens. Thus, *monandrous, diandrous, triandrous, tetrandrous*, and *polyandrous*; from the Greek words "*monos*," one, alone; "*dis*," "*duo*," double, two; "*tris*," "*treis*," three; "*tetra*," from "*tessares*," four; "*polūs*," many; and "*androus*," stamens.

(iii.) Or again, after the Greek words "*prōtos*," "*prōteros*," first, before, in *protandrous* or *proterandrous*, which mean that the stamens ripen or mature before the pistil (p. 130).

Atmosphere.—From the Greek "*atmos*," vapour, and "*sphaira*," sphere, meaning the air which surrounds the earth.

(i.) It is almost entirely made up of three gases, *nitrogen, oxygen*, and *carbon dioxide* (carbonic acid gas). Out of 100 portions or volumes, about 79 would be nitrogen, and not quite 21 would be oxygen, the remainder being chiefly carbon dioxide.

(ii.) Carbon dioxide or carbonic acid gas is composed of two parts of oxygen and one part of carbon.

(iii.) Carbon is a solid and elementary substance, that is, chemists have not found it to be a composition of other substances. You can easily see it, for the black lead of a common pencil is carbon. Pure crystallized carbon is very valuable, as the beautiful diamond. Under certain conditions carbon unites with oxygen gas, and so forms carbon dioxide, or carbonic acid gas.

Carbon.—See Atmosphere iii.

Carbonic Acid Gas.—See Atmosphere ii.

Cell.—Sometimes, as in the formation of pollen, the nucleus of the mother cell divides into four parts, around each of which the protoplasm gathers, and a cell wall forms, so that each becomes a new and perfect cell.

When the nucleus of a mother cell divides into many parts, or new nuclei, each becoming surrounded by protoplasm before new walls are formed, it is called *free cell formation*. This takes place in the formation of the endosperm in the embryo bags of ovules.

See chlorophyll corpuscle dividing, in Fig. 163, b, b', b''; and endosperm cells which are being formed by free cell formation in Fig. 113 S, p. 134.

Collar.—The part at which the stem ends and the root begins.

Cortex.—Used collectively of that which is outside the cambium; and so including (i.) the phloem or bast (secondary cortex), and (ii.) the fundamental tissue, etc., which is outside the bast (primary cortex). Sometimes used to mean the part outside the bast only (primary cortex).

Dehiscence.—When a capsule splits or opens by the separation of its carpels, *i.e.*, down the dissepiments, the dehiscence is *septicidal*,[*] or splitting down the septa or dissepiments. When, however, the carpels split open down the dorsal suture, the dehiscence is called

---

[*] From the Latin "*septum*," the partition or dissepiment, and "*cædo*," I cut.

loculicidal,* or splitting open down the loculi. But sometimes in a multilocular capsule (p. 119) the dissepiments remain joined to the axis, the outside capsule wall splitting off from them by the carpel pieces or valves. This kind of dehiscence is known as *septifragal*,† or breaking away from the septa or dissepiments.

In fruits or fruitlets of a single carpel, when it dehisces along ventral or dorsal suture or both, the dehiscence is *sutural*.

Diffusion.—If a liquid is in contact with a thicker or heavier liquid, its tendency will be to diffuse into or mix with it. A very thin skin may be between them, and yet the movement will go on. If two different gases are so separated, they also pass through and intermix. So different liquids and gases can pass through the very thin walls of the cells and vessels of plants, and the sap changes, moves, and travels.

Endosperm.—This food substance is called Endosperm or Perisperm, according to its position.

If it is in the embryo sac or inner bag of the ovule (Fig. 113 S, p. 134), it is called *endosperm*, from the Greek "*endon*," within, and "*sperma*," the seed. See Fig. 136 B, marked E; it sometimes fills the whole testa, Fig. 136 A, marked E.

But in Fig. 136 B is an instance of a seed with the (inner) endosperm E, surrounded by the (outer) *perisperm*, which fills up the rest of the nucellus (*cf.* under funicle) and is marked P.

Perisperm is from the Greek "*peri*," around, and "*sperma*," seed. Compare Figs. 113 and 136 B; S of Fig. 113 corresponds with E of Fig. 136 B; *k* of Fig. 113 with P of Fig. 136 B.

Funicle.‡—This is the stalk by which the ovule may be attached to the placenta. (Fig. 178 *f*).

The ovule is made up of one or two coats or coverings (integuments), inside which is a cellular mass or substance called the *nucellus* § (Figs. 109 S, p. 129; 178 *k*); and in the nucellus is

---

* From the Latin "*loculus*," the box or pocket, and "*cædo*," I cut.
† From the Latin "*septum*," as on page 222, and "*frango*," I break.
‡ From the Latin "*funis*," a cord.
§ Connected with "nucleus," from the Latin "*nux*," gen. "*nucis*," a nut, the kernel; "*nucellus*," a little kernel, or nucleus.

the *embryo* or *germ sac*, a cell containing the *germ* (Figs. 109 *e m E*; 178 S, E). The integuments do not entirely cover the nucellus, but at one place a narrow passage is left between them. This is called the *micropyle* *; and through this the pollen tube passes in fertilisation, after it has come down the stigma, until it reaches the embryo sac and fertilises the germ, or *oosphere*,† as it is called. (*cf.* Fig. 178).

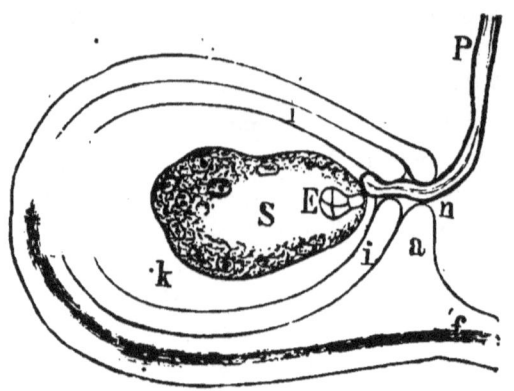

FIG. 178.—Ovule shortly after fertilisation. *k* nucellus, with S, embryo sac; E, embryo which has begun to grow from the fertilised oosphere; *a*, outer, *i*, inner integument; *f*, funicle; *n*, micropyle; *p*, pollen tube.

Gland.—A cell containing or separating from the sap, some oily or other special substance. *cf.* glandular hairs, p. 82, 81 Fig. 54.

Gynous.—Used in composition with other words, and refers to the pistil. It is from the Greek "*gunē*," gen. *gunaikos*, a woman.
(i.) So the pistil is also called "*Gynœcium*," or "*Gynœcœcium*," from the Greek "*gunaikos*," as above, and "*oikion*," a house: the woman's house.
(ii.) Used sometimes (as androus is) of the pistil carpels, ovaries, styles, or stigmas. *Digynous*, etc., see Androus ii.
(iii.) So also *protogynous* or *proterogynous*, when the pistil matures before the stamens. *cf.* Androus iii.

---

* From the Greek "*mikros*," small, and "*pulē*," a gate.
† From the Greek "*ōon*," an egg, and "*sphaira*," a globe or ball; the egg ball.

Hermaphrodite.—Flowers which have both stamens (men, *cf.* androus) and pistil (woman, *cf.* gynous) are called *hermaphrodite.* From the Greek "*hermaphroditos,*" an effeminate man, both man and woman; from "*Hermes,*" Mercury, and "*Aphrodite,*" Venus. A flower with only stamens or pistil, not both, is accordingly called "*unisexual,*" of one sex. Sometimes hermaphrodite flowers, as well as stameniferous (p. 122), or pistiliferous (p. 122) flowers, are found upon the same plant, such a plant is described as *polygamous.*

Monochlamydeous.—When a flower has only calyx or corolla, it is called *monochlamydeous,* from the Greek "*monos,*" one, and "*chlamys,*" a cloak or mantle : it has only one cloak or garment. When it has two garments, calyx and corolla, it is *dichlamydeous,* from the Greek "*dis,*" twice, double, and "*chlamys,*" as above. When it has neither calyx nor corolla, the flower is *achlamydeous,* from the Greek "*a,*" not, and "*chlamys,*" as above : it has no garment.

Monomerous.—In describing the ovary as to the number of carpels of which it is made up, the Greek word "*meros,*" a share or part, is used instead of carpel, with a Greek numeral placed before it to denote the number of the carpels or parts of which the ovary is made up. Thus "mono" (*monos,* one); "poly" (*polus,* many); or more particularly, "di" (*dis, duo,* two); "tri" (*tris,* three); "tetra" (*tessares,* four); "penta" (*pente,* five); and "merous" (*meros*); monomerous, dimerous, etc. Thus, pistil syncarpous, ovary pentamerous (5-carpelled). These words, monomerous, etc., are used of other parts of a flower also.

Nectary.—The word has been generally used of the cavities or places on various parts of plants, where the sweet fluid is found, which is called *nectar,* or flower honey. The nectary is properly the glandular (p. 82*) portion or substance from which the nectar oozes (which secretes the nectar). See nectary scale at base of petals of celandine, buttercup, or grass of parnassus, also the glandular nectariferous expansions or swellings (disc) on floral receptacle (as in *Rhamnus*). The various positions of the nectaries in flowers are very interesting in connection with the visits of insects and the work they do in pollination (p. 129).

Perisperm.—See Endosperm.

Parasites, Saprophytes.—Some flowering plants have no chlorophyll, and so they cannot take in carbon by assimilation. They are consequently obliged to take their carbon, which is necessary to their life, combined with something else, that is, as I have called it, prepared food (p. 200). When they do this from other living plants, they are called *parasites*. If they take it from the decayed remains of plants they are called *saprophytes*. The mistletoe has green leaves and is only partly parasitic (p. 75).

Placentation means the way in which the ovules are attached or placed within the ovary. This varies with the different kinds of ovaries, and you will understand the different kinds of placentation more easily if you remember that the ovules are usually upon the margins of the carpel leaves.

(i.) So if the ovary be simply monomerous and unilocular, since the ovules are upon the margins of the carpel leaf, they are just inside and along each side of the ventral suture (p. 116). Their placentation or attachment is therefore described as *marginal* or *sutural* placentation (Fig. 102 A, p. 119).

(ii.) But now suppose the ovary is polymerous and unilocular. Here the margins of the carpel leaves simply join, as in Fig. 102 B, p being their junction, that is the placenta. Or the carpel leaves may be turned in so as to form a unilocular but chambered ovary (p. 119), as in Fig. 102 C, p showing the placenta. In this case, as the ovules are upon the walls or partial dissepiments of the ovary, their placentation is called *parietal* * placentation.

(iii.) But if the ovary is polymerous and multilocular, then the dissepiments reach the centre of the ovary, as in Fig. 102 D, and the placentas p are upon a central column or axis. In this case, because the ovules are thus upon the axis, the placentation is called *axile*.

(iv.) If in a polymerous multilocular ovary the dissepiments fall away, the ovules are left upon the axis in a unilocular or chambered ovary. Their placentation is then called *free central* placentation.

---

* From the Latin "*paries*," a wall.

The same term is used when the ovules are upon a raised column or projection from the receptacle into the ovary, without connection with dissepiments or carpels.

Thalamus.—Same as the torus or receptacle. It is from the Greek "*thalamos,*" an inner room or chamber.

Saprophyte.—See Parasite.

Sarcocarp.—Another term for the mesocarp when it is pulpy or fleshy. From the Greek "*sarx,*" gen. "*sarkos,*" flesh, and "*karpos,*" fruit.

Sclerenchyma.—Cellular tissue of which the walls of the cells are more or less thickened and hardened. It is from the Greek "*sklēros,*" hard, and "*encheo,*" I pour in ("*enchyma,*" tissue).

APPENDIX B.—LEAVES.

Rachis.—That part of the lengthened petiole or peduncle, along which are arranged the leaflets of a compound leaf, or the flowers of an inflorescence, as the case may be.

From the Greek "*rachis,*" the backbone.

Pedatifid.—Used of a palmatifid leaf (*simple*, p. 95), when the two side divisions are again indented or cleft.

The word is derived from the Latin "*pes,*" "*pedis,*" a foot; and is used from a fancied resemblance of a leaf so divided to the foot of a bird.

Pedate.—(Same derivation). Used in like manner of a palmately *compound* leaf when the two side leaflets are deeply lobed or cleft.

Sometimes the clefts are so deep that they reach into the petiole, and the divisions are themselves leaflets.

Capillary.—Used of a finely-divided leaf. Hair-like; from the Latin "*capillus,*" hair.

Multifid.—Much divided; from the Latin "*multus*," much, a "*fid*" (p. 95*).

Phyllode.—In some plants the leaf stalk becomes widened and flattened, so that it looks like a blade (p. 89). Such an expanded petiole is called a *phyllode*; from the Greek "*phullon*," a leaf, and "*eidos*," form.

Sometimes there is the Phyllode only, but sometimes the true blade can be seen growing at the end of the Phyllode.

Cladophyll.—This is not a leaf, like the Phyllode, but a *branch*, widened, flattened, and leaf-like.

You can see an example of it in the Butcher's Broom (*Ruscus aculeatus*). The small scale-like leaves, from the axils of which the cladophylls grow, soon wither and fall off, so you should look for them upon young stems.

The word is derived from the Greek "*klados*," a young branch or shoot, and "*phullon*," a leaf.

The cladophyll is also called "cladode" ("*klados*" and "*eidos*") and "phylloclade" ("*phullon*" and "*klados*.")

Oblique or **Unsymmetrical** leaves are those of which the two halves are not alike or equal; as in the elm.

APPENDIX C.—Fruits.

Caryopsis.—This is the name given to the fruit of the grasses. It is similar to the achene (dry, indehiscent and one seeded), but the pericarp is inseparable from the seed, which is not the case in the achene.

In some grasses, as in oats and barley, the paleæ (p. 102) adhere to the caryopsis. Derivation from the Greek "*karuon*," a nut, and "*opsis*," appearance.

Cypsela.—This is an inferior achene, and you have examples of it in the fruit of the compositæ (Fig. 138 *e*, p. 159). To distinguish the flowers of the compositæ, *cf.* p. 47, 48, and remember that they have an inferior ovary, and five stamens, which are joined together (*cf.* Fig. 138 *d* and its note, p. 159). Cypsela is derived from the Greek "*kupselē*," a box, a hollow vessel.

Samara.—This is a dry one seeded fruit or fruitlet, similar to the achene, but with a membranous margin or wing formed by the extended pericarp. See the winged achene or samara of the elm (Fig. 131 B, p. 146), and the winged mericarp or samara of the sycamore (Fig. 28 *b*, p. 33). It is from the Latin "*samera*," the seed of the elm.

Coccus.—A fruitlet of a schizocarp when they are more than two in number; from the Greek "*kokkos*," a kernel, a berry (Fig. 141, p. 161). The one seeded fruitlets of the schizocarp are similar to the nut or achene. With a glass that magnifies about twenty times, look at transverse sections from those of some of the common labiates (p. 42, 109).

But compare a coccus of the labiates or of the geranium family with an achene, that of a buttercup for instance, as to their dehiscence. In the geraniums you can easily see the dehiscent carpel of the coccus, in contrast with the indehiscent achene.

Berry.—The fruit of the cucumber, melon, and vegetable marrow is somewhat different from the true berry. Part of the pericarp is thicker, fleshy, and more or less hard, and the seeds do not lie loose in the pulp, as in the true berry. A fruit of this kind is called a "*pepo.*"

Pome.—A succulent, indehiscent syncarpous and spurious fruit such as the apple or pear, *cf.* p. 29, 136. From the Latin "*pomum*," an apple.

Sorosis.—When the flowers of an inflorescence, by the swelling of some of their parts, produce one succulent collective fruit, as the pine-apple, it is called a *sorosis*. Another instance is the fruit of the mulberry, produced by the swelling of the perianth leaves (p. 139*).

The word sorosis is derived from the Greek "*sōros*," a heap, an accumulation.

Syconus (from the Greek "*sukon*," a fig) is a collective fruit, such as that of the fig. (See p. 138.)

INDEX.

PAGE	**PAGE**
A in Composition, *cf.* Monochlamydeous 225	Arum. See Lords and Ladies.
Absorption ... 192	Asparagus.. ... 67
Acacia ...(plate) 201	Assimilation... 197
Achene ...146, 159	Atmosphere ... 221
Achlamydeous, *cf.* Monochlamydeous... 225	Avens, Common... 86, 215
	Awn ... 102
Acicular ... 91	Axil ... 78
Acorn......103, (plate) 135, 137, 147	Axis ...65, 70
Acropetal Succession ... 79, 84	
Acute ... 94	
Adventitious 74, 80	Balsam, Yellow ... 160
Aerial Roots ...66, 75	Banyan ... 75
Ailanthus ...(plate) 181	Bark ......18, cells of (plate) 170; 173, 180 to 182
Air Spaces ...169, 183, (plate) 194	
Almond......fruit (plate) 140	Barley ......(plate) 102, 125, 126
seed (plate) 154	Bast ... 177 to 180, 222
Amentum ... 125	Bean...stipules, 99; fruit, 116, 137, 140, 144; seed, 64, 71, 153, 154, 185
Amplexicaul ... 98	
Anagallis—See Pimpernel ...	
Anatomy ... 60, 164 to 189	Bean, Indian ... 205
Andrœcium—See Androus i. ... 221	Beak ......(plate) 161
Androus ... 221	Beech......nut, 103, 137, 147; leaf (plate) 87, 194
Anemone...17, 68, 74	
Anemophilous ... 130	Beet-root ......root (plate) 14; 186
Angiosperms ... 210	Begonia, leaf-stalk ......(plate) 184
Annuals ... 205	Berry... 149, 229
Annulated ......74, vessels 168	Bi in Composition ... 97½
Anther ......112, (plate) 129, 190	Biennial ... 205
Anthriscus—See Cow Parsley.	Bijugate ... 97
Apex. The tip or top end.	Bilocular ... 119
Apocarpous...pistil 116; fruit 137	Bindweed......rhizome, 68, 74; flower, 110
Apple............fruit (plate) 28, 135, 229; seed 152; leaf 193	
	Birch ......(plate) 76
Apricot ......fruit 140, 148	Bipinnate ......97, (plate) 201
Arillus ...... (plate) 207, 209	Bird's Foot Trefoil...(plate) 37, 39, 46
Aristolochia ...(plate) 132	
Artificial System of Classification ... 216	Bird's Foot ... 143
	Biternate ... 96

PAGE		PAGE
Blackberry...29, fruit 137, 139, (plate) 148, 215		Celandine, Greater 187
Blackthorn 80		Celandine, Lesser ...(plate) 89, 225
Bloom 188		Celery 202
Botany... 2, 3; branches of, 59 to 62		Cell, 165; wall, 166; sap, 166; division, 167, 222; contents 183
Bract... 100; involucral, 103, 111		
Bramble—See Blackberry.		Cellular tissue 167
Branching 78		Cellulose, a substance of which the cell wall is composed.
Brassica, ovary (plate) 118; fruit (plate) 141, 144		Cerastium—See Mouse-ear Chick-weed.
Brazil nut 155		
Bryony 65		Chambered Ovary 119
Buds 76		Charlock 38
Bud scales 77, 104, 105		Chelidonium—See Celandine, Greater.
Bulbs... .15, 17, 68, 74, 104, 199		
Buckthorn ... .. (plate) 117, 225		Cherry, 29, 48; fruit (plate) 140, 142, 148
Bulrush ....fruit 160		
Burnet-leaved Rose......(plate) 27		Chestnut, Horse 104, 105
Butcher's Broom 228		Chestnut, Sweet 103
Buttercup, Meadow, 5, (plate) 6, 49, 110		Chlorophyll................... 184, 202
		Chlorophyll Corpuscle, 184,185, 197, 199, 222
,, Tuberous (Bulbous), (plate) 4, 6, 49		Chrysanthemum 67
,, Creeping 49, 74, 110		Ciliate 94
,, pistil, 27, 116; ovary, 118; fruit, 137, 140, 146		Cinquefoil......................... 111
		Cladode 228
		Cladophyll 228
		Class 32, 209
Caliculus 111		Classification......32 to 49, 61, 207 to 218
Calycifloral 216		
Calyx 6, 53, 107		Clavate............................. 81
Cambium ....177 to 180		Claw 108
Campanulate 109		Cleavers 162
Capillary 227		Clematis 160
Capitulum 126		Climbing Stem............ ... 18, 65
Capsicum ....(plate) 128		Clover 17, 40, 46, 61
Capsella—See Shepherd's Purse.		Coccus 229
Capsule................................... 145		Colchicum—See Crocus, Autumn.
Caraway ....(plate) 147		
Carbon 197, 199, 203, 222		Collar 222
Carbon Dioxide 195, 196, 198, 221, 222		Collecting Plants... 53
		Collective Fruit 138
Carbonic Acid Gas—See Carbon Dioxide.		Columbine . ...fruit, 137, 144
		Colour 131
Carpel ....114 to 117		Coltsfoot ....100, (plate) 213
Carrot ....(plate) 99, 215		Composite 48, (plate) 159, 213, 229
Caryopsis 228		Compound Leaf 22
Catkin 125		,, Umbel 43
Cauline. 86		,, Fruit 137, 138
Caulis, an aerial stem 107		Cone................................ 125

	PAGE
Connate	98
Convolvulus	18
Cordate	92
Core	29
Cork ....52, (plate)	181
Corm 68,	74
Corolla 5,	107
Corollifloral	216
Corpuscle—See Chlorophyll.	
Cortex ....177 to 182,	222
Corymb	125
Cotton Grass	160
Cotyledon.... 33, 54, 64, 154,	210
Couch Grass 68,	74
Cow Parsley ...44, 103; stem,	184
Cow Parsnip, (plate) 44; ovary, 118; fruit, 147,	215
Cowslip (plate) 1, fruit, 137, 141,	145
Creeping Stem 17,	66
Crenate	94
Cress ....(fruit)	145
Crocus	69
Crocus, Autumn, 69; fruit (plate)	145
Cross fertilisation ......130 to	133
Crown	67
Cruciferous 37,	108
Cryptogam 2,	207
Crystal 186,	199
Cuckoo Pint—See Lords and Ladies.	
Cucumber ...ovary, 118; fruit,	149
Culm	84
Cupule	103
Currant, flower, 125; fruit, 140, 142,	149
Cuticle	172
Cyme	126
Cynoglossum—See Hound's Tongue.	
Cypsela 159,	229
Dahlia root, 14; crown, 67; tubercles, 73; pith,	167
Daisy.........(plate) 46, 47, 103,	126
Damson ......29; stone (plate)	170
Dandelion ...flowers, 48, 110; root, 71; involucre, 103; fruit, 158; (plate) 159; juice,	187

	PAG
Date...(plate) 151; fruit, 140, 149, 152,	155
Dead Nettle (plate) 41, 85, 109,	110
Deadly Nightshade..(plate) 50,	51
Deca in Composition, from the Greek "*deka*," ten.	
Decandrous, *cf.* Deca and Androus.	
Deciduous, falling off, from the Latin "*de*" down, and "*cado*" I fall............53,	54
Decumbent	66
Decurrent	98
Decussate	85
Deferred Growth	79
Dehiscent. Dehiscence...141, 145, 153,	222
Dentate	94
Di in Composition	176
Diadelphous. Stamens in two bundles or brotherhoods (Fig. 15 c); from the Greek "*di*" (*cf.* above) and "*adelphos*" a brother	21
Diandrous, *cf.* Androus ii.	221
Dichlamydeous, *cf.* Monochlamydeous	225
Dicotyledon 33, 176,	210
Dictamnus..............(plate)	188
Didynamous. Of four Stamens, one pair being longer than the other pair. From the Greek "*di*" (*cf.* above), and *aunamis*, power.	
Diffusion	223
Digitate	97
Digynous, *cf.* Gynous ii	224
Dimerous, *cf.* Monomerous	225
Diœcious	123
Disc	126
Discifloral	215
Dissepiment 119,	144
Dock ....(plate)	195
Dorsal Suture ......116, (plate)	119
Double Flowers	112
Draining	204
Dropwort	73
Drying Plants	54
Drupe	148
Drupel	148

	PAGE		PAGE
Earthnut	45	Foxglove (plate) 32,	125
Economic Botany	62	Fragaria—See Strawberry.	
Elder 109, pith 167,	174	Free Cell Formation, *cf.* Cell	222
Elliptical	91	Fruit 26 to 31 ; 134 to	150
Elm fruit (plate)	146	Fruitlet	139
Emarginate	93	Fuchsia	67
Embryo 64, 134, 154,	224	Fundamental Tissue 174,	222
Enchanter's Nightshade ...fruit	162	Funicle	223
Endocarp 139,	170	Funnel Shaped	110
Endogens	211	Furze—See Gorse.	
Endogenous 179,	211	Fusiform	71
Endosperm 191,	223		
Entire	93		
Entomophilous 130 to	133	Galium—See Cleavers.	
Epicalyx	111	Galls	52
Epicarp	139	Gamo in composition	109
Epidermis 172, 181 (plate),	194	Gamopetalous	109
Epigynous 215,	216	Gamosepalous	110
Epipetalous	216	Gases 191, 195 to	198
Exogens	211	Genus 46 to 48,	217
Exogenous 179,	211	Geographical Botany	62
		Geranium (plate)	161
		Germ 64, 71,	224
		Germination	190
Fascicle, Fascicled, Fasciculated. From the Latin "*Fascis*," a bundle of rods. In a cluster or bundle.		Gill-run-along-the-ground—See Ground Ivy.	
		Glabrous	82
Fertilisation	133	Gladiolus	69
Fennel (plate)	70	Gland 82,	224
Fibril	73	Glandular	82
Fibrous (Fibre) 51, 72,	173	Globose	71
Fibro-vascular bundles 173, 175 to	180	Glume	102
Fid in Composition	95	Gooseberry, ovary, 118 ; fruit, 142,	149
Fig fruit (plate) 138, 140,	230	Goosegrass—See Silver Weed.	
Filament	112	Gorse 24, 40, 47 ; fruit,	144
Fir pollen, 130 ; fruit, 125, 138 ; (plate) 139 ; resin (plate) 188 ;	212	Gourd	149
		Grape 140,	149
		Grass, 50; stem, 89, 184 ; flower, 101, 102, (plate)	171
Flag	68		
Flax	180	Grass of Parnassus	225
Flora	217	Green	202
Floret 48, 126, (plate) 159,	213	Ground Ivy .... 17, (plate) 18,	74
Flower 4 to 11, 77 ; leaves, 111 ; double, 112 ;	118	Gum	188
		Gymnosperm	209
Follicle	144	Gynandrous	216
Food of Plants 191, 192,	201	Gynœcium. See Gynous i.	224
Food Store 154, 191,	199	Gynous	224
Fool's Parsley (plate)	157		
Fossil Botany	62		

INDEX.

	PAGE
Hairbell	110
Hairs	23, (plate) 81, 171
Harriff	23; fruit, 162
Hastate	92
Hawthorn	80
Hazel, scale, 101; cupule, 103, (plate) 121, 123; flowers, 122, 125; pollen, 130; nut, 29, 140, 142,	147
Heat	190, 194, 203
Hedge Parsley	fruit, 162
Hellebore	leafstalk (plate) 174
Hemp	180
Henbane	fruit (plate) 146
Hepatica	111
Herb, Herbaceous	18
Herbarium	55
Herb Bennet, cf. Avens, Common.	
Herb, Robert, fruit, 147, (plate)	161
Hermaphrodite	225
Hip	28, 135, 136, 140
Histology	60
Honeysuckle	(plate) 59, 85
Hooker	205, 218
Hop, flowers, 123, (plate) 124; fruit,	138
Hornbeam	103
Horse Chestnut, 77, 85; bark cells (plate)	170
Horse Radish	67
Hound's Tongue	162
Hyacinth, bulb, (plate) 68, 104; (plate) 114; crystals	186
Hyoscyamus—See Henbane.	
Hypericum—See St. John's Wort.	
Hypogynous	214, 215
Impatiens—See Yellow Balsam.	
Imparipinnate	97
Incomplete Flowers	122
Indehiscent	142
India Rubber	188
Indian Bean	205
Inferior Ovary	118
Inflorescence	124
Insects and Flowers	131 to 133
Integument	223, 224
Intercellular spaces	169, 183, 188
Internodes	84

	PAGE
Involucel, the bracts or involucre of an umbellule, cf 103,	126
Involucel, 103, (plate) 106, 126,	213
Involute, with the margins turned in, see note	103
Ipecacuanha, (plate) 12; root, 14,	74
Iris	68; fruit, 141
Iron	191
Ivy	75
Juniper	212
Kecksie—See Cow Parsley.	
Keel	39
Knot Grass	(plate) 100
Labiate	41 to 43, 109
Ladies' Mantle	88, (plate) 87
Lamina	89
Lanceolate	92
Larch	fruit 125
Larkspur	fruit 144
Lateral	78
Lavender	67
Layering	74
Leaflet	22, 96
Leaf	21 to 25, 83 to 105; floral, 111 to 114; venation, 34, 95, 173; drooping, 194; (plate) 194
Leaf scales	104, 105
Legume	30, 108, 143
Leguminosæ — See Papilionaceous	108
Lemon	fruit, 149; scent, 188
Life	190; seeds, 205; plants, 205
Light	194, 202, 203
Ligulate	89, 110
Ligule	89
Lilac	bud, 77; flower, 109; stomates, 193
Lily	68, 104
Lily of Valley	68, (plate) 190
Limb of Corolla	108, 109
Lime	100, 105, (plate) 178
Linear	91, (plate) 106

	PAGE		PAGE
Linnæus 40,	216	Monopetalous, of one petal—	
Linnæan Classification	216	See "Mono" and "Petal."	
Lipped—See Labiate.		Monosepalous, of one sepal—	
Lobed	94	See "Mono" and "Sepal."	
Loculicidal Dehiscence	223	Morphology...........................	60
Loculus.................................	119	Mouse-ear Chickweed...flower,	
Lomentum 143,	145	126; fruit, 141,	145
Lonicera—See Honeysuckle.		Mucronate	99
Lords and Ladies......fruit, 51; spathe, 101; flowers, 123, 124; (plate)	175	Mulberry......fruit, 138, (plate) 139,	230
		Multi in Composition............	119*
Lotus—See Bird's Foot Trefoil.		Multifid................................	228
Lubbock 160,	162	Multilocular.........................	119
Lychnis...petal, 109; fruit, 145; seed,	153	Mustard...seed, 33; flower, 38; fruit,	144
Lyrate	96	Myrtle	188
		Names of Plants...................48,	217
Mallow ....(plate) 7,	111	Napiform	71
Malva—See Mallow.		Natural Order 35,	214
Maple—See Sycamore.		Natural System of Classification 32 to 36, 207 to 216,	217
Manure	204		
Margin	93	Nectar	131
Marrow — See Vegetable Marrow.		Nectary...............................	225
		Nettle, Stinging 51, 68,	173
May—See Hawthorn.		Net Veined Leaves ... 35, 211,	212
Medulla—See Pith.		Nitrogen 191,	221
Medullary Ray	179	Node..................................	83
Melilot ....fruit (plate)	116	Nodose, or Nodulose	73
Mericarp	147	Nucellus 223,	224
Mesocarp	139	Nucleus..............................	166
Metabolism	199	Nut	146
Metastasis	199	Nutmeg...............................	155
Micropyle	224	Nutrition, Organs of ......63 to	105
Mistletoe.......................75,	226	Nux Vomica.........fruit (plate)	154
Monadelphous. Stamens in one bundle—See "Mono" and "Diadelphous."		Oak, galls and bark, 52; fruit, 103, (plate) 135; ovary, 147; wood (plate)	176
Monandrous	221		
Moniliform	73	Oat........................(plate)	125
Monkshood...fruit, 137, 141, 144, (plate) 117, (plate)	183	Obcordate...........................	93
		Oblanceolate	93
Mono in Composition	176*	Oblique Leaves	228
Monocarpous	204	Oblong	91
Monochlamydeous	225	Obovate	93
Monocotyledon ...34, 72, 176,	210	Obtuse	94
Monœcious	123	Ochrea	100
Monogynous, cf. Gynous ii. ...	224	Oil 188,	199
Monomerous	225		

INDEX.

	PAGE
Onion	68, 104
Oosphere	224
Opium	187
Orange, fruit, 30, 149, 165; seed, 152; scent,	188
Orbicular	91
Order, Natural—See Natural Order.	
Organs—See Nutrition and Reproduction.	
Ornithopus—See Bird's Foot.	
Oval	91
Ovary	115 to 119, 128
Ovate	92
Ovule...115, 119, 133, (plate) 134, 223, (plate)	224
Oxlip	(plate) 131
Oxygen ...191, 197, 198, 221,	222
Palea	102
Palm	(plate) 151
Palmate Leaf	87, 95
Palmately lobed	95
,, Compound	96
Palmate venation	87
Palmatifid	95
Palmatipartite	95
Palmatisected	95
Panduriform, same as Fiddle-shaped	23
Panicle	125
Pansy Violet......stipules, 99; fruit (plate)	160
Papilionaceous	39, 40, 108
Pappus	158, 159
Parasite	75, 226
Parenchyma	167
Paripinnate	97
Partite in composition	95
Pea, (plate) 21, 38, 99; fruit, 116, 137, 141,	144
Peach ......fruit, 140, 148, 170,	174
Pear ....seed, 152,	229
Pedate	227
Pedatifid	227
Pedicel	107
Peduncle	107
Peltate	93
Penny Cress	145

	PAGE
Penny Wort	93
Penta in composition, *cf.* Monomerous	225
Pentamerous, *cf.* Monomerous	225
Pentandrous—See Penta and Androus.	
Pepo	229
Perennial	205
Perfoliate	98
Perfume	131
Perianth	111
Pericarp	139, 153, 158
Perigynous	214 to 216
Perisperm	226
Personate	109
Petal	36, 108
Petiole	89
Petiolule, a secondary petiole.	
Phanerogam	208
Phænogam	208
Phloem—See Bast.	
Phlox	67
Phylloclade	228
Phyllode	228
Phyllotaxis	85
Physiology	61, 190 to 206
Pig-nut	45
Pimpernel........fruit 141,	146
Pine	125, 212
Pine Apple	139, 229
Pink	108
Pinnæ	97
Pinnate Leaf	97
Pinnate Venation	88
Pinnatifid	95
Pinnatipartite	95
Pinnatisected	95
Pinnules	97
Piper	(plate) 154
Pistil	9, 114 to 118, 128
Pistiliferous	122
Pith	19, 167, 170, 174, 179
Pitted Vessels	168
Placenta	120
Placentation	120, 226
Plantago—See Plantain.	
Plantain...124, fruit, 146; leaf,	173
Plum.........fruit 140, 148, 152,	174
Plumule	65
Pluri in Composition	

	PAGE
Pod ......4, (plate) 21, 30, 116,	143
Pollen 112, 129, 131,	133
Pollination 129,	130
Poly in Composition	108†
Polyadelphous. Stamens in many bundles—See "Poly" and "Diadelphous."	
Polyandrous, *cf.* Androus ii. ...	221
Polycarpous	205
Polycotyledonous	210
Polygamous, *cf.* Hermaphrodite	225
Polygonum—See Knot Grass.	
Polymerous, *cf.* Monomerous...	225
Polypetalous	108
Polysepalous	110
Pome.............................	229
Poppy...fruit (plate) 30, 137, 140, 141, 146; (plate) 143, seed, 156; juice,	187
Pore	141
Pore Capsule ....(plate) 30,	146
Potato...tuber, 69; roots, 74; starch, 185; shoots, 202,	203
Potentilla—See Silver Weed.	
Prantl 132,	219
Prickle	80
Primrose.. 10, 16, 68; flowers, 109, 110, 131; pistil, 117; ovary, 118; fruit, 137, 141,	145
Primula—See Primrose, Cowslip, and Oxlip.	
Privet ....(plate) 83,	85
Procumbent	66
Prosenchyma	168
Prostrate	66
Protandrous, *cf.* Androus iii....	221
Proterandrous, *cf.* Androus iii.	221
Protogynous, *cf.* Gynous iii. ..	224
Protoplasm 166, 178,	184
Pseudocarp	135
Pubescent........................	82
Pyxidium	146
Quadri in Composition	96
Quadrinate	96
Quinate...........................	96

	PAGE
Raceme...........................	125
Rachis	227
Radical Leaves 21, 53,	86
Radicle...........................	71
Radish...38; fruit, 140, (plate)	145
Raphides	187
Raspberry, stock, 67, (plate) 26; fruit, 29, 139,	148
Ray	126
Receptacle, 107, (plate) 117, 126, (plate) 159,	213
Reniform	93
Reproduction, Organs of ...63,	106
Resin..............................	188
Respiration	198
Rhamnus—See Buckthorn.	
Rhizome 67, 74,	199
Rhubarb, crown, 67; stem, 100, vessels, (plate) 169; raphides,	187
Rice.......................... 50,	185
Ringed Vessels	168
Ringent...........................	109
Rings of Trees ....176 to	179
Root, 12 to 14, 70 to 75; uses of, 15,	24
Root-hairs ......(plate) 34, 73,	191
Root-leaves 21, 53,	86
Rose, 52, 80; fruit, 28, 136, 140,	146
Rotate	109
Rotundate	92
Runcinate.......................	96
Runner...........................	66
Rush ....(plate) 63,	184
Rush, Flowering ....(plate)	106
Saffron Crocus ....(plate)	16
Saffron, Meadow.................	69
Sagittate ....92, (plate)	175
Salver-shaped	109
Samara 146,	229
Sambucus—See Elder.	
Sand Sedge ....68, (plate)	67
Sap 20, 24, 192, 198,	223
Saprophyte......... 75,	227
Sarcocarp........................	227
Scalariform	168
Scale ...7, 101, 104, 105, 122, (plate) 123,	124

INDEX. 239

	PAGE
Scandent	65
Scape	106, 107
Scaly Bulb	68
Scent	131
Schizocarp	147
Sclerenchyma	170, 227
Scotch Fir, 130; seed (plate), 160; resin (plate),	188
Sea Kale	67, 202
Sected in composition	95‡
Seed, 64, 70, 120; formation of, 128 to 134; 151 to 156; distribution of, 157 to 163; growth of, 32, 190; vitality of, 205,	208
Self Pollination	130
Self Fertilisation	130
Sepal	110, 111
Septicidal, *cf.* Dehiscence	222*
Septifragal, *cf.* Dehiscence	223†
Septum	222*
Serrate	94
Sessile	90
Setæ	81
Setose	82
Sheath	89
Shepherd's Purse	38, 145
Silicula Silicle	144
Siliqua	144
Silver Grain	179
Silver Weed	111
Simple Leaf	22
Simple Fruit	137, 138
Simple Pistil	117
Sinuous	94
Siphonia	juice, 187
Skeleton Leaf	173
Sloe—See Blackthorn	29, 80
Snapdragon	109, 146
Snowdrop	68
Soboles	66, 68
Solomon's Seal	68
Sorosis	229
Spadix	124, (plate) 175
Spathe	101, 124, (plate) 175
Spathulate	93
Species	48, 49, 217
Speedwell	109
Spermaphyte	208
Spike	102, 124, 125

	PAGE
Spikelet	102, 126
Spindle-shaped Root	71
Spine	24
Spiral Vessels	168
Spurious Fruit	135
Spurge	187
St. John's Wort	188
Stamen	9, 112, 215, 216, 221
Stameniferous	122
Standard	39
Starch	185, 197, 199
Stem	16 to 20, 63 to 69, 73, 167
Stigma	115, 128, 172
Stipule	99, 111
Stock	67
Stolon	66
Stoma, Stomate, 25, 193, (plate)	194
Stone Crop	(plate) 53
Stone Fruit...148; cells, (plate)	170, 174
Stork's Bill	161
Straight-veined Leaf	35
Strawberry...runner (plate), 66; fruit, 27, (plate) 28, 111,	136, 146
Style	115, 128
Subulate	92
Succulent Fruits	140, 148
Sucker	80
Sugar	186
Sunflower	(plate) 177, 194
Superior Ovary	118
Suture	116
Sweetbriar	23
Sycamore...(plate) 33, 34; bud, 77, 104, 105; fruit,	160
Syconus	230
Syncarpous	pistil, 114, 117; fruit, 137
Syngynesious, "Joined together," from Greek "*sun*" with, and "*genesis*" "*geno*"	179*
Systematic Botany	61
Tap root	71
Teasel	126, (plate) 164
Temperature	190, 194, 203
Tendril	18, 24, 66
Ternate	96

| | PAGE | | PAGE |

Testa ....152 to 154, 158
Tetra in Composition — See Androus ii. 221
Tetrandrous, *cf.* Androus ii. ... 221
Tetradynamous, when of six stamens, four (two pairs) are longer, and two (one pair) shorter.—See "Tetra" and "Didynamous."
Tetramerous, *cf.* Monomerous 225
Thalamifloral 215
Thalamus 107, 227
Thistle ....(plate) 91, 103, 160
Thlaspi—See Penny Cress.
Thorn 80
Thyme 74
Tissue ....167 to 174
Tomentose 82
Torilis—See Hedge Parsley.
Torus 107
Transpiration 192
Tri in Composition 96
Triandrous, *cf.* Androus ii. ... 221
Trigynous, *cf.* Gynous ii. 224
Trijugate 97
Trilocular......119, (plate) 114, 190
Trimerous, *cf.* Monomerous ... 225
Tripartite 95
Tripinnate 97
Trisected 95
Triternate 97
Tube of Petal 109
Tuber 69, 73, 191, 199
Tubercle 73, 199
Tubular Corolla 110
Tulip ....68 ; ovary, 118
Tunicated Bulb 68
Turnip................(plate) 10, 205

Umbel 43, 44, 126
Umbelliferous ....43 to 45
Umbellule 126
Uncinate 81
Uni in Composition 119*
Unilocular ovary 119
Unisexual, *cf.* Hermaphrodite 225
Use of Plants ....50 to 53, 200

Valve.............................. 141
Vascular Tissue............169, 173
Vegetable Marrow 149, 215
Venation ......34, 35, 86 to 88, 173, 175
Ventral Suture ......116, (plate) 119
Veronica—See Speedwell.
Vessel 168
Vetch 140
Vine—See Grape 18
Violet 129
Violet, Pansy—See Pansy Violet.

Wall-flower, ovary, 118; fruit, 141, 144
Walnut, fruit, 148, 174 ; seed, 152, 153, 155
Water-cress ....(plate) 74
Water Lily ....fruit, 149
Wheat, 72, (plate) 102; flower 126; 185
Whitethorn—See Hawthorn.
Whitlow Grass............(plate) 144
Whorl 85
Willow, stipules, 99, (plate) 100; flowers, 123, 125
Willow Herb, ovary, 118; pollen, (plate) 133 ; fruit, 160
Wind Pollination................. 130
Window Plants 203
Wing.............................. 39
Winged............................ 98
Wood, cells, (plate) 167, 175 to 182
Woodruff ....(plate) 85

Xylem—See Wood.

Yellow Balsam.................... 160
Yew, flowers, 123; pollen, 130, (plate) 207, 209

Bemrose & Sons, Printers, Derby; and 23, Old Bailey, London.

BY THE SAME AUTHOR.

BRAVE MEN OF OLD.

Twelve Easy Readings on the Twelve Minor Prophets.

For Bible Class and Sunday School Teachers, or for Sunday Reading at home.

Paper Boards 1s. 6d., Cloth 2s.

"... They give us a succinct account of the scope and contents of each book and a vivacious picture of the men and their times."—*Oldham Chronicle.*

"A brief description of the general scope of each prophet's writings. ..... good of its kind."—*Church Times.*

"A thoroughly valuable book, bringing together a mass of interesting information ... Plain readers of the Bible will find this volume a real help, and we heartily recommend it.—*Fireside News.*

"... They may be of service in whetting the appetite for larger works, or in helping to a more intelligent study of these too much neglected books of the Old Testament."—*Nonconformist.*

"It professes to give a brief account of each of the minor prophets with the characteristics of their works, and carries out its purpose very fairly; a good deal of information being compressed in its 120 pages, and sermonising being sparingly introduced."—*Literary Churchman.*

PREPARATION AND THANKS-GIVING
FOR HOLY COMMUNION.

Two Short Services arranged from the Bible and Book of Common Prayer.

For Communicants' Meetings or as an addition to Family Prayers for Communicants.

16 pages in wrapper, post free 2s. per dozen. Specimen, Two Stamps.

Extracts from notices of the Press on Flower Land, Part 1.

—— :o:——

"Gives in some sixty pages the main facts of the science in a very simple and attractive form. It may be put into the hands of children, or used as a guide by those who have to teach them, without in the first instance knowing anything of the subject. It will be found excellent for either purpose."—*Guardian.*

"The aim of this little work is as simple as its method of treatment. . . So far as it goes, it is the very alphabet of botanology; we have nothing but praise to accord to it."—*Naturalist.*

"We recommend the book highly."—*Natural History Journal.*

"This little volume is, according to the double preface, intended as a guide both to those beginning to learn botany, and to those who would instruct them. . . The author has avoided long scientific and Latin words as carefully as possible, which makes the book quite readable for the young; and, as the subject matter is thoroughly sound, it will prove useful for our little friends. . ."—*Literary World.*

"Few books are written in such a plain manner as this, especially when dealing with botany. It is one of the easiest introductions to that subject we have come across; in fact the author has made it so simple that it can be perused with advantage by all in the first stage of botany. It is well written. . ."—*Horticultural Times.*

"The various parts of the flower, root, stem and leaf are treated of in an easy and popular way, the intention being to put into the hands of teachers an easy method of giving instruction to children in the rudiments of the science."—*Gardening World.*

"The idea is a good one."—*Manchester Guardian.*

"Science made simple and interesting; real and substantial knowledge conveyed in an attractive manner. . . The bright and chatty style of the author must make him a charming companion to the young folk; and the information given will help many to spend happy hours in 'Flower Land.' . ."—*Fireside News.*

". . . The language of the work is beautifully clear and simple, and perfectly suited to the capacities of those to whom it is addressed. Parents and teachers who are able to take their children for country rambles will find here a capital basis provided for conversational lessons in the rudiments of Botany. We like the book very much. . ." —*Teachers' Aid.*

"'Flower Land' is a simple introduction to the study of Botany, for the use of young children, parents, and teachers. It is simply written and attractive in style. . ."—*School Guardian.*

"We like this little botany book. The simple, terse, 'taking' style in which its instructions are conveyed ought to render them palatable, as well as profitable, to youthful students."—*Church Bells.*

www.ingramcontent.com/pod-product-compliance
Lightning Source LLC
Chambersburg PA
CBHW020800230426
43666CB00007B/780